CITIZEN SHANE

By Tom Romita

The economic and political information in this book is factual to the best of the author's knowledge.

The information regarding Orlando Bloom is not.

CHAPTER 1

"Imagine no possessions
I wonder if you can
No need for greed or hunger
A brotherhood of man
Imagine all the people sharing all the world..."

-John Lennon

It's a typical night at Lucky's Bar, crown jewel of the Prospect Heights section of Brooklyn. The crowd is a mix of hipsters and hipsterettes—some in work clothes, some not. For several, it's hard to tell. There are a few in business wear, and a smattering of blacks, Hispanics, and Asians. The place reeks of gentrification, entitled bitterness, and muddled bitters.

Twenty-seven-year old Shane Foster holds court behind the bar. He's the Grand Poobah, the high priest, the embodiment of all that the bar and those in it stand for. Shane is good-looking, privileged, and strategically dressed to convey abject poverty. Scoffing the establishment is his modus operandi and his religion. He is the pinnacle, the shining example of how this cadre of New York twenty-somethings wants to be: successful, happy, and popular, with the air of absolute ambivalence to his privilege and good fortune. Even Shane's hair is a deceptively organized arrangement of curated chaos.

"Wait until you try this," he proudly says to a few friends gathered at the bar.

Sam is twenty-six, with slicked-back, dirty blond hair that makes him look more grease monkey than Gordon Gekko. He's wearing a suit that badly wants to be an Armani, and shoes that are almost Pradas. He loosens his tie, which is pink, and disappointingly not a Zegna. He watches as Shane uses a muddler to crush and combine a mysterious potion in a small bowl. It appears to be the makings of a trendy, old fashioned-style cocktail.

"What is that?" Sam asks.

"It's a secret," Shane answers.

"It's weed."

"It's not weed," Shane says disdainfully, still muddling.

"It smells like feet," says Gio, a twenty-eight-year old African-American guy with short dreadlocks and a "Living Colour" t-shirt everyone is hesitant to ask him about. He turns up his nose and grimaces at the concoction. Shane stops muddling and looks up at Gio indignantly.

"It's not feet. Will you just shut up and hold on a minute?"

Zora, a twenty-six-year old free spirit of a girl who looks as comfortable and attractive in a ball gown as she does in her current choice of jeans and a t-shirt, giggles at the ritualistic posturing behavior of the Brooklyn Male. She pulls a lock of brown hair behind her ear and watches Shane with pale green eyes as he transfers the mixture into a cocktail shaker. Shane looks up at her and smiles. He adds some golden liquid from a glass bottle and shakes, then reaches under the bar and pulls out a plastic spray bottle that looks like it should contain kitchen cleanser. He unscrews the top and pours the amber mixture from the shaker into it.

"Dude?" Gio says, as Zora scrunches her nose in mild disgust.

"Ew," she says.

Shane stops pouring, looks at his three friends. "Guys, I cleaned it," he says, in his best annoyed-father voice. "There's no Windex or Jagermeister in the spray bottle. Re. Fucking. Lax. Do you think I'm trying to kill my three best customers before you close your tab?"

They laugh and smile, still slightly wary, as Shane screws the spray top back on. He slides over to the food pick-up area at the far end of the bar and returns with a small, mixed green salad. He proceeds to spray a generous amount of the golden elixir on the salad, and pushes it, along with three forks, toward Sam, Gio, and Zora. They look at each other hesitantly. Zora shrugs, bravely grabs a fork, stabs a tomato slice, and pops it into her mouth. Sam and Gio follow suit.

"Holy shit," Sam says, as the forkful of concoction-coated greens engages his taste buds.

"Mmmm," says Gio, tongue tingling with savory delight. "Damn."

"Oh my God," Zora says in zest-induced ecstasy.

"It's good?" Shane asks.

Gio stops munching for a moment to reply. "Dude. It's like… damn," is all he's got.

"It's so zesty and tangy," says Sam. "It's zangy."

"I want to drink this," Zora says.

"I want to shower in this," adds Gio.

Shane is smiling proudly. "I just used a lot of the stuff we use in the bartisan drinks here," he says. "Traded the booze for extra virgin olive oil, and bam!"

"You should sell this stuff," says Sam. "Seriously."

Shane looks at his happy friends and thinks about what Sam said, and how fucking stupid it was. He's never understood why, whenever anyone has a great idea, pens a fabulous book, creates a catchy song, writes a riveting screenplay, paints a beautiful portrait, builds an inspiring sculpture, or invents an awesome new product, there's always a mad dash to sell it. That just turns any beautiful creation into something ugly—a business, a commodity, a means of profit. Money screws everything up. People want more of it so they can buy more things that businesspeople convince them they need, so that *they* can make more money by selling stuff. It's a symbiotic system of American ugliness that he wishes would just end. Why couldn't people be more like him and just appreciate a creative accomplishment for what it is?

"No thank you," he says, emphatically. "Just the smiles on those beautiful faces are enough for me!"

"Aw, you're so sweet," Zora says, patting Shane on the hand.

"Whatever," says Sam. "You should sell this shit."

Shane bites his tongue and shakes his head, tapping a beer for a customer.

"There are certainly plenty of places around BK to do it, if you wanted to," adds Gio. "Everyone's got their own damn beer, coffee, pickles. Why not salad dressing?"

"Spritz," says Shane.

"What?"

"It's not dressing," says Shane, picking up the spray bottle. "Dressing you pour. Spritz you… spritz." With a flourish, he adds some more to their salads.

"You are a tool," says Sam. "But it's really freaking good."

From the far end of the bar, a tan guy with a white tank top and unbuttoned pink oxford bellows at Shane, "Yo! Who do I have to blow to get a Bud Light around here?" His similarly adorned buddy laughs loudly and slaps him on the back, as if he's just won an Olympic event.

Shane looks up, then says to his friends, "Sorry, got a situation to deal with over here."

"Looks like you have 'The Situation' to deal with over there," Gio says.

"You can almost smell the Axe from all the way over here," Sam says.

"One B&T, coming right up!" Shane yells to the guy, who looks confused. Gio, Sam, and Zora giggle. "Salad's on me," Shane says to them, as he moves down the bar. "And the next round. I'll be back."

"Careful with the Roids Scholars," Zora says, smiling, as Shane approaches the tanned twosome.

Gio takes a bite. And another. "Damn," he says, treasuring every tangy morsel. "And I don't even like salad."

Later, Shane is alone in the bar, cleaning up at the end of a busy shift. It's 3 AM. He hates this part of the job. He reminds himself to talk to Henry, the owner, about hiring a service to do the cleaning. The bar's making money, so why shouldn't he get some more help? Henry's a good guy, but like all business owners, he has a greedy streak that bothers Shane sometimes. He often suffers silently while Henry proudly talks about opening another bar, like he's having another child. He can never understand why successful businessmen don't leave well enough alone. You've got a successful business. You are done. Enjoy it!

But businessmen always want more. More money. More material things. The greed drives him crazy. Why continue to struggle, to risk, to sacrifice, when you've already succeeded at what you set out to accomplish? Do you really need a yacht that you can land a helicopter on? Whether it's a bar, a hotel, a manufacturing plant, Amazon.com, it's all the same thing. You start a business, and if you're lucky enough to be successful, just be satisfied with what you've got. Use your profits to pay for what you need and keep running your successful business. Simple.

As Shane is finishing the glasses, he grabs the spray bottle that holds the salad spritz. It's nearly empty. He needs to start another batch tomorrow to get ready for Zora's upcoming potluck party. As he's typing a reminder into his smartphone, a young couple enters the front door. They're dressed for an upscale party, and pretty drunk. Shane instantly regrets forgetting to lock the door.

"Oh, hey," he says to them, not completely unfriendly. "We're closed."

"Oh man," the drunk guy says. "I thought you were open till four?"

"Sorry, not tonight," Shane says, barely looking up from his phone.

"Did the hours change?" the girl asks.

Shane looks up, annoyed.

"Nope," he says. "Just closing early, since there's no one here."

Shots fired.

"Get home safe," he says.

"We've got a limo outside," the guy replies. "Can we just have one drink? We won't even bother you." He motions to a table away from the bar. "We'll sit right here."

"We were at a charity event," the girl says, giggling. "We forgot which one was tonight. It was for an alcohol rehab facility in Park Slope. There was no alcohol! Who knew?"

"Had to sneak in a flask like a peasant!" the guy says, laughing. "We have the sitter for another hour. One drink?"

Shane looks disdainfully at them.

"Sorry. Can't help you," he says.

"I'll give you fifty bucks," the guy says. "We'll be done before you finish cleaning."

Shane scoffs and goes back to his phone. "Sorry," he says. "Have a good night."

"Shit," the guy says. "Okay, fine."

"Neighborhood's changed," the girl says, looking at Shane. "Later."

She stumbles out of the bar, and the guy follows. Shane watches them go, and hurries to lock the door behind them.

"Rich pricks," he mutters to himself.

Fifteen or so friends are milling about Zora's small but comfortable apartment in Clinton Hill. Its décor is a vibrant menagerie of flea market chic, parental funds, and Ikea. Like its tenant, the place is not exquisitely beautiful, but its effortless, unpretentious charm is similarly appealing. The guests are eating and discussing the various potluck artisanal dishes they've brought, all of which currently reside on a large, clothed folding table in the center of the living room. Gio and Sam are there, sampling the offerings. Zora is chatting with some friends while anxiously checking the time on her phone. The door buzzes and she scurries off to answer it.

"Where have you been?!" she asks, opening the door. Shane is standing there, flustered, balancing six spray bottles of his spritz and various other culinary supplies in two hands, with the futile assistance of a few holey plastic grocery bags.

"God. Sorry," he says. "They didn't have cilantro *or* cumin at the co-op. I had to go all the way to Scheinman's. Sorry. Can you…"

Zora grabs three of the bottles from Shane.

"Get in here. I've been telling everyone that your spritz stuff is to *die* for."

"Ugh, ok. Can I have a minute to-"

"No!" Zora cuts him off, smiling, takes him by the hand, and leads him inside.

They enter to a chorus of mock cheers and jeers. Shane apologetically dispenses the bottles around the table amongst the artisanal treats.

"I hope this is worth the wait," someone says.

"Oh, it is," says Gio. "Trust."

"Seriously, that stuff's no joke," adds Sam. "Shane, thanks man, you can go home now."

"Screw you," Shane says. Everyone laughs as they grab bottles and start herbally enhancing their small-batch quinoa, heirloom beets, and cruelty-free chicken salads. Soon, the 'oohs' and 'ahhs' and compliments begin to flow as freely as Shane's spritz from Lucky's repurposed spray bottles. Zora looks at Shane. He shrugs, and smiles.

Later that night, Shane, Gio, and Sam sit around Zora's living room, a little drunk, smoking a joint. The rest of the evening's guests are gone.

"Capitalism doesn't work," Gio is saying as he takes a hit off the joint. "We tried. It failed. Look at this country. Everyone hates us. We're like, fortieth on the world literacy list. We're below Uzbekistan, for fuck's sake. Our health care sucks. The greedy banks fucked it all up. Time to move on."

He passes the joint to Sam, who takes a hit.

"Move on to what, G?" Sam asks, exhaling. "Socialism? You know what socialism relies on? Government-controlled public education. The same kind that has made us dumber than Uzbekistan."

"I don't know," Gio says. "You can't possibly think letting rich, greedy businessmen make all the decisions is a good idea?"

"Well, I don't think that being rich means you're necessarily 'greedy.' And I don't know that being greedy is necessarily the worst thing to be. Greed motivates people to do good as well as bad."

"Well, someone needs to make sure that the greedy bad ones don't take over the joint," Gio says. "Cuz you know they will."

"And that 'someone' would be our politicians. How are they doing? Want to give them *more* power? If you really think those shitheels in Washington are looking out for *your* well-being, well, that's some good shit you're smoking." He passes the joint to Shane. "Right, Shaney? Democrat or Republican?"

Shane takes a hit. "No idea," he says. "I don't think about politics."

"It's not politics," Sam says. "It's life."

"You gotta care a little, man," Gio says. "It's pretty easy to pick a side. Democrats want everyone to be financially comfortable, educated, and healthy, and Republicans are racists."

Sam shakes his head at his black best friend. "Or, Republicans understand that governing a nation means more than just promising everything to everyone, and that making tough decisions that might piss some folks off is part of the job. Perhaps they understand that every nation has unique, limited resources that you have to figure out the smartest thing to do with."

"That's not life," Shane says, scowling as he passes the joint back to Gio. "Capitalism, socialism… Republican, Democrat… that's some people deciding where the money goes. Life isn't about money. As long as I have enough to buy a round for my friends, fuck everything else. What's that make me?"

Sam says, "A Republican" at the same time Gio says, "A Democrat."

Their laughter is broken by the sound of what could definitely be gunshots from the street outside the apartment. It's not close enough to send them diving for cover, but not far enough away to ignore.

"Jesus, there are too many guns around," Gio says, taking another hit. "They should be completely banned in the city."

"They are," says Sam disdainfully. "So are drugs."

Gio looks at the joint in his hand and shrugs. "That's different," he says to Sam.

"Yeah," says Sam. "You like drugs. You hate guns. That's not basis for municipal policy. People should be allowed to have guns."

"Do you have a gun?" Gio asks Sam defiantly.

"No," Sam answers. "But I do have a brain."

Shane smiles and shakes his head.

"McNeil and Lehrer at it again?"

The guys look up to see Zora in the archway between her kitchen and living room, drying a salad plate with a dish towel. Shane smiles at her.

"Yeah," he answers, slightly confused. "I think McNeil's winning." Then pointing to Sam, he asks, "Wait, which one's which?"

"Sam's McNeil," Zora says.

"Oh. Then Lehrer's winning."

"Fuck off, hippie," Sam says, as Gio grins.

"Shane," Zora says, "if you can leave your refereeing duties for a minute, I could use a hand in the kitchen."

"Okay," he says, and gets up from the couch. He and Zora leave the room as Gio and Sam exchange glances.

"That mean what I think it means?" Sam asks.

"Oh yeah," Gio answers. "It's on."

Shane and Zora barely get out of Gio and Sam's line of sight before they're against the refrigerator, kissing.

"That was a great party," Shane says.

"Thanks. Your spritz was a hit. Everybody wants some."

"They can call Paul Newman. I almost died making all of that," he says, twisting his hand in a circle. "I think I have carpal tunnel. That ginger root doesn't muddle itself, you know."

"Aw, too bad," says Zora, giggling. "I could use a back rub."

Shane looks her in the eye, smiles, and moves his hand to her back. "I think it's improving."

He kisses her again and caresses the small of her back. Zora leads him by the hand out of the kitchen towards her bedroom, oblivious to Sam and Gio's presence.

"We'll just let ourselves… see you tomorrow… we're all good," mumbles Gio.

Sam shrugs and takes a hit from the joint.

CHAPTER 2

Shane reluctantly opens an eye that has just been struck by a cruel streak of sunlight, blazing a path through Brooklyn's skyline and navigating the space between Zora's curtains. Zora sleeps next to him, her eyes safely out of the light's attack line. The light hits her tawny brown hair, igniting an unwieldly mane that spills over her white pillow. Shane opens the other eye, groggily sits up, and looks at her.

She's gorgeous, he thinks. That much is obvious. Not in a traditional way, necessarily, not sultry, not "hot," but with all of her parts in all the right places, arranged in a way that makes you want to smile and hug her for a few hours. He then finds himself having another thought, one mostly foreign to him: that this person he has just spent the night with is a good person. A smart person. A strong woman. He sees her less like a conquest, and more of an accomplishment. As he looks at her, he feels differently about himself, about his life, about who he is. He's proud—not that he "got laid," but that he did so with this fantastic woman. He smiles, thinking about how much he'd like to do it again; then, slightly startled at where his heart has wandered, he lifts the sheet and lets his eyes wander to her perfectly round ass to stave off the fleeting moment of maturity.

"My God," he mutters to himself.

He drops the sheet gently, so as not to awaken her, and grabs his cell phone from the nightstand. "What the actual fuck," he groans, looking at it, scrolling and swiping. Zora stirs.

"What's the matter?" she asks.

"Oh, sorry. Nothing. Sleep."

"I'm up," she says, sitting, stretching, and forcing her eyes to function. They land on Shane. He's certainly cute, for a hipster, she thinks. A bit typical, one of the legions of guys trying so hard to look unique that they wind up looking like everyone else trying to do the same. Ironically unironic, ironically. She normally doesn't go to bed with guys this early in a relationship. She "normally" doesn't go to bed with them at all. Shane was the guy who completed the hand on which she could count the number of guys she'd slept with. She was certainly far from falling for him, and she got the feeling that as long as she didn't, he wouldn't hurt her. He was a perfect boyfriend, especially in the sense that boyfriends, unlike fiancés and husbands, were temporary. She wasn't ready to settle down, and she couldn't imagine Shane ever would be either. But besides being cute and gentle and funny, she couldn't help feeling there was more to this scruffy, blue-eyed bartender. He seemed to have all the elements necessary to become a great man, but didn't know exactly how to manage them properly, or how lucky he was to possess his natural looks and charm. While she knew better than to try to change or mold him—or any man, for that matter—into her own image, she didn't think there would be any harm in trying to cultivate some of these admirable qualities in Shane, and seeing what might grow. If she succeeded, settling down could be on the table in the future. The far future.

"I have eighteen e-mails," Shane says, flustered, looking at his phone. "Nine people want the salad spritz. Five want the recipe, and three want to know where they can buy some."

"That's seventeen," Zora says.

Shane scrolls down further and stops.

"Marissa says she had an erotic dream about it."

Zora giggles and curls up next to him. "That's great," she says. "Isn't it?"

She'd seen what wasted potential fully realized looked like in her father, a decent writer of books and poems, all forever entombed in notepads, file cases, and floppy discs. Her mother, the financial analyst and breadwinner, always insisted that he follow his passions while she kept the lights on. She said she would love him whether they ever paid off or not. But after twenty years of perceived failure, the unwavering love his wife provided couldn't overcome the festering hate he felt for himself. He put down the laptop and bottle of bourbon long enough to book a one-way ticket to Mexico, never to return to his wife and daughter. The day he left, Zora's mother asked what he was going to do there, and he said one word, "Write."

"Ugh. I mean, I'm glad they like it," Shane says, "but I don't have time to make all this. It's not like it's what I do. I'm a bartender."

Zora looks down, strokes the edge of the white sheet, and pulls it around her a little. While she didn't feel deeply scarred from her always-distant father's departure, she assumed his example, along with her mother's mantra, "Follow your passions, but get a job," had a lot to do with her leaving Indiana for the New York literary agency where she worked. It also may have explained her unwavering desire to not see potential go unrealized, or at least unexplored. Especially in those she slept with.

"Maybe you're a salad spritz maker," Zora offers lightly. "You're apparently very good at it."

"But I just want, I don't… Christ, now I'll look like an asshole if I don't make more."

"Just give them the recipe," Zora says sympathetically.

"I can't," Shane says, slightly exasperated. "It's a little complicated. There are certain spices that are only in specific stores, different ones at different times of year, even depends on the week sometimes. You have to mull some, muddle others… some you put in early, some later, depending on what you've got. Sometimes, I have to substitute stuff that's not in season, and that changes the whole recipe. I know what works from mixing drinks for five years. I sorta wing it a bit, but it always seems to work. It's fun in small batches. But in volume, it's a giant pain in the ass."

Zora never thought she would get turned on by a guy espousing his passion for mulled spices. But there she was, tingling.

"I get it," Zora says, thinking. "Maybe you could get help?"

"Help? For what? I don't even want to do this."

"Okay," Zora says, pulling the sheets up around her tighter and leaning against the wall behind her.

"What?" Shane asks.

"No. It's just…" Zora pauses. She thinks of the fun night they just had, and how well things were going with Shane. She was not sure she wanted to ask the next question, and navigate the minefield she may be about to step into. She wondered what her father was doing in Mexico. Probably drinking. She braces, and takes the step.

"What *do* you want to do?" she asks.

"I don't know," Shane answers quickly. "I like working at Lucky's."

"I know," Zora answers. "But I mean, like, forever?"

"I might go to culinary school. Eventually."

"New York restaurant business is tough," Zora says. "Wolfgang Puck won't even come here."

Shane shifts in the bed, suddenly having trouble getting comfortable. He puts his phone down.

"Zo, we've been seeing each other for like three weeks," he says. "Why am I feeling career pressure?"

"No. Not at all," Zora says, realizing she pushed a bit too hard. "This really has nothing to do with me, or us, or what I might want or not want. I'm thinking about what would make you happy, even if we aren't together. I'm just saying, as a friend, or whatever, if you have an opportunity, maybe look into it."

Shane has that feeling again. This is a good person he's in bed with. A good person that he couldn't disagree with any more.

"I'm not interested in opportunities in salad dressing," Shane says glumly.

"Spritz," Zora says.

Shane shoots her a look. She smiles wryly. He tackles her and they fall onto the bed, giggling.

Later, Shane is pouring white wine into glasses for two ladies who are in for a quick bite at the bar. They're in their late twenties, and each have a plate of pasta primavera in front of them. Henry, the owner of Lucky's, is milling around behind the bar, taking inventory. The ladies are poking at their meals, looking as uninspired as the dishes in front of them.

"Here you go, ladies, two Pinot Grigios," Shane says. "Get you anything else? Primaveras okay?"

"They're okay," one of the ladies says politely.

"Sorry," Shane says. "The usual guy is off tonight and I'm not sure Ivan has his flair for the Italian. Wines are on me."

"Thanks," the other lady says. "I mean, they are fine. Just a little meh."

Sam and Gio stroll in and settle at the bar next to the ladies.

"'Sup, Shane," Sam says, and then notices the two attractive ladies next to him. "Ladies," he says with an unintentionally goofy smile. "I'm Sam. That's Gio."

"Hannah," says one, holding out her hand.

"Claudia. Hello," says the other.

"Nice to meet you guys," Gio says. "What you up to, Shane?"

"Oh, just buying a round for these lovely ladies."

"Ivan in the kitchen again, huh?" Sam asks. Hannah and Claudia laugh. Shane scowls at him.

"Dude, shut up," he says.

"I'm kidding. Sort of. I hear he makes great… borscht."

"Ooh, you serve borscht here?" Claudia asks.

"No," Shane says.

Henry, wiping his hands with a bar towel, sidles over to the group. He's a little overweight and underheight, always sweaty and extremely sociable. He didn't play football at Rutgers, but was in the football fraternity anyway.

"Sam, Gio, ladies," he says. They all nod and say hello. "Shane, you good?" he asks. "I'm gonna bust out a little early. Kid's got a fever. Or the house is on fire," he says, shrugging. "Wife's cell phone crapped out halfway through the call."

Gio's eyes widen as Sam, Claudia, and Hannah stifle laughs.

"Either way, you should probably go," Shane says, rolling his eyes and smiling.

"Right? I figured," Henry says. "Yeah. Okay, I'm out. Ciao, y'all," he says as he heads for the door.

"Good luck," Gio says, smiling. He notices the ladies poking at their pastas. "Hey, Shane, you got any of that spritz stuff?"

"Yeah. I started another batch today," Shane says. "Everybody wants some. Why?"

"Throw some on!" Gio says.

"What?" Shane asks. "The pasta?"

"Why not?" Gio says. "From the looks on Hannah and Claudia's faces, you've got nothing to lose."

"It's not that bad," Claudia says politely. She takes a bite and frowns a little. "Spritz?" she asks.

"Yeah, oh man, this stuff's insane," Sam says. "Come on, ya extra virgin, bust some out!"

"All right, all right," Shane says, and asks the ladies, "Can I try something? If you don't like it, I'll have the kitchen make you something else. I promise, okay?"

Hannah and Claudia look at each other.

"Sure," Hannah says.

Shane pulls out a spray bottle.

"It's not bar cleaner, I swear," he says, spraying a little into his mouth. The ladies giggle. He sprays some on their pastas. They take a bite.

"Oh," Hannah says, chewing. "Oh, my. What is that?"

"Wow," Claudia says. "Hit me again!"

"You have *got* to be kidding me," Shane says, bewildered.

He sprays a little more on both of their dishes, then addresses the guys. "What do you guys want?"

"Two Goose Islands," says Sam.

"And two pastas," adds Gio.

Shane shakes his head, smiles, and taps the beers.

The bar empties out early that night, even for a Tuesday, and by 12:30AM, Sam and Gio are keeping Shane company as he cleans up, in return for free beer. The conversation goes to where New York City conversations go far too often—the rent, and how to pay it.

"It just sucks, man," Sam says, taking a sip. "I mean, I'm glad for Sean, he's a good guy, but I have some apps that are just as good as his. But he's got the three-bedroom in Tribeca from his parents, who got it from their parents. No rent, no mortgage, nada. He rents one of the bedrooms out for a grand a month! So he can sit home all day and figure out who he should take to lunch and pitch his apps to. Me, I have to go to work every day and keep stockbrokers' terminals running to pay for my shitty studio in Murray Hill."

"Tell me about it," says Gio. "I'm grinding and grinding in the studio, getting jingles rejected for friggin' online condom ads, and two other composers from my NYU class are home waiting for movie gigs to come along. Waiting! Imagine that."

"How can they do that?" asks Shane.

"One's got a rent-controlled loft in Soho, and one's got a rich girlfriend," Gio says.

"I need one of those," Sam says.

"Which?" asks Gio.

"Either," says Sam. "Doesn't matter."

"You guys worry too much about money," Shane says. "It's not worth the stress. Make enough to get by, what else do you really need? We live in a world where we think we need a lot more than we actually do. Fucking advertising. It's bullshit they're selling. Makes everyone crazy. And greedy."

"Dude," Sam says, looking disapprovingly at Shane, then hitting him with aggressive air quotes. "'Getting by' in Brooklyn is fun for now, but life gets expensive, man. Bushwick's still affordable, but just wait. New York neighborhoods all follow the same progression: poor, artsy, cool, trendy, gay, beautiful, hot, yuppie, rich, unaffordable."

"Well, Bushwick's still at artsy-cool, so I've got plenty of time," Shane says.

"If it stays that way, you probably won't want to live there when you're thirty-five."

"And you gotta watch out for the gays, man," Gio says emphatically. "They come in and clean up hoods like motherfuckers. They straight up skipped artsy, cool *and* trendy in Hell's Kitchen. Shit went from ghetto to gorgeous overnight, I'm telling you. Look out or your hipster ghetto pad is on StreetEasy for $3500 a month, and Jeffrey and Timothy will rent that shit up. Trust."

Shane shakes his head as they all take a drink.

"Let's be honest," Sam says. "We're pushing thirty. People settle down later in the city here, but I think we all would like to, someday, right? At the rate I'm going, I'll be sixty before I'm financially stable. And you, mister hot shot, you ain't gonna be such a hit with the ladies slinging drinks at sixty."

Shane takes this in. "I'm not worried about money," he says.

"There are two kinds of people who don't worry about money: the ones that don't have to," Sam says, "and the ones that should."

"Something will happen," Shane says, trying to keep positive.

"There are two ways 'waiting for something to happen' turns out," Sam says. "Lucky and rich, or unlucky and homeless. Riding high at the Ritz or fluffing for BangBros in Atlantic City. I'm not waiting to find out. I'm going to try to make shit happen. Fuck luck."

"Truth," Gio says. "What pisses me off is that I *am* trying to make shit happen. Grinding, man. I'm good at what I do, and I have nothing to show for it. That blows."

"I just need a break. One big break," Sam says. "Sean's looking for investors. It's pretty much a sure thing. Google is looking at his apps. He's gonna be like Zuckerberg.

I could get in on that action, if I had more than four hundred and thirty- three dollars in the bank."

Shane feels a genuine concern for his friends, and the future. He taps three more beers.

"On me," he says.

CHAPTER 3

"Zo!" Shane calls to Zora, who's checking out a table full of small batch mustards. "Try this beet root chutney. It's amazing."

Smorgasburg is a weekly outdoor food extravaganza that takes place in the Williamsburg section of Brooklyn every Saturday, weather permitting. Twenty years ago, if you were white and in Williamsburg, you were in one of two places—Peter Luger's steak house, or a cab going to Peter Luger's steak house. Much has changed in Williamsburg since then: the demographics, the price of real estate, and the food. Known as the "Woodstock of Eating," Smorgasburg became a mainstay in Williamsburg about the same time the first wave of bearded hipsters and urban soccer moms settled into the shiny new high-rises along the East River. Hundreds of vendors pack the East River State Park every Saturday to hawk the hottest, trendiest artisan provisions. Shane and Zora move through the various vendor tents, perusing and sampling a veritable cornucopia of hand-crafted treats.

Zora joins Shane and tastes a sample.

"Wow. How much?" she asks the buck-toothed, moustache-and-buzzcut-sporting vendor. He would look like a pedophile, or a displaced Slav, if it weren't for the enormous plastic pink neon shades.

"Eleven dollars," he says.

"For *one* jar?" Zora asks, taken aback.

"It's organic," the vendor says, dismissive and bored behind his Hello Kitty eyewear.

"Are there inorganic beets?" she asks.

The vendor sighs, pulls out his phone, and begins swiping furiously. "It's gluten free. Dairy free. Small batch. Non-GMO. Cruelty free."

"Are people being cruel to beets?" she asks.

Shane pinches her arm lightly. The vendor looks up momentarily, then turns his attention back to Tinder.

"Locally sourced?" Shane asks.

"No," the vendor says with a proud smile. "Imported."

"Oh. From where?" Zora asks.

"Indiana," says the vendor.

"Okay, thanks," says Shane, as Zora takes his hand and leads him away. The vendor scowls and goes back to heavily petting his phone.

"This place is amazing, isn't it?" Shane says. "Holy shit, is that the Massey Brothers coffee over there? Look at the line!"

Zora looks over at the throngs of rapturous counterculture caffeine mavens and can't help but wonder why they would line up to pay double for a bag of "exotic imported" coffee that has always been brought in from places like Colombia, Sumatra, Kenya, and Java.

"It's a fun place to hang out," Zora says, as they stroll through the maze of tents. "But it's such a smoke show."

"What do you mean?" Shane asks.

"It's like one guy after another trying to 'out organic' the next," she says. "With all the talk these days about safe, healthy foods, somehow people are competing to sell and buy the most primitively produced, unregulated stuff for people to put in their bodies."

They see a vendor advertising and handing out samples of "Line-Caught Whitefish. Locally Sourced." A small crowd of yupsters gather to get their free chunk of sea-being.

"I've seen that guy fishing under the bridge," Shane says. "Don't taste that."

"Is any of this even legal?" Zora asks.

"Who knows," Shane says. "I don't think the FDA cares too much about the Brooklyn food scene. They're busy making sure Monsanto doesn't turn us all into GMO zombies."

"Seriously. Hey, did you hear about the 'Caliente' chain?" Zora asks. "The 'organic' Mexican place that serves fifteen-dollar tacos?"

"Yeah," Shane says. "They started here, right? They were opening a new one every month for a while. What happened?"

"The FDA started requiring that restaurant chains display calorie counts on their menus."

"So?"

"Well, contrary to popular belief," Zora says, "organic doesn't necessarily mean low calorie. Or even healthy. I mean, animal fat and sugar are organic."

"Ah. Okay."

"So the Caliente folks had to get creative in order to keep their customers from seeing what they were actually eating. A chain, by definition, is fifteen of the same restaurants." She pauses to sample a beer-brined pickle. "Did you notice the 'Caliente' on West 68th became a 'Muy Caliente,' and the one in the Village became 'Casa Caliente,' and then a 'Caliente Grande' opened in Union Square, all with a pretty much identical menu?"

"Yeah, I remember that," Shane says. "I was wondering how those places got away with that. They're a total rip-off."

"Because it's not a rip-off," Zora says. "It's the same owners. Same restaurant. New names."

"What? No."

"Yep. Different names for the new ones mean there are only *fourteen* 'Caliente' restaurants in New York, which means they aren't a chain, which means—"

"No calorie counts required on the menus."

"You got it," Zora says. "They're expanding faster than ever. Just in disguise."

Shane looks at Zora. He's enjoying receiving something he never had from a beautiful woman before: knowledge.

"They would really do that, just to avoid displaying calories?" he asks.

"Do you think people would line up around the block for an 'organic' fifteen-dollar taco if they knew it was packing fifteen hundred calories?" Zora asks.

"Wow. I think not," Shane says. "I guess it's kind of a crapshoot." He gestures to the whitefish vendor. "Might as well eat the Hudson's finest scrod."

"I have no idea what you should or shouldn't eat," Zora says. "Well, I guess besides McDonald's."

"I guess," Shane says. He thinks a moment and adds, "But, I mean, look at a lot of professional athletes. They're from poor urban and rural areas and have grown into our ultimate examples of strength and fitness. These kids didn't grow up eating truffles at Jean George. They were probably noshing a lot of McNuggets."

Zora mulls it over. "Suddenly I want a Big Mac," she says, longingly.

Shane looks around. "That guy has free range yak burgers," he says, gesturing toward a nearby bearded gentleman's tent.

"Close enough," Zora says, as they head in that direction.

They approach the yak burger vendor, who could be an Alsatian logger were it not for the nose ring.

Zora stops short as they approach. "Jacob?" she says, recognizing the lumbersexual purveyor of yak.

"Hey! Zora! How are you?" he says enthusiastically, giving her a friendly hug.

"I'm good. Good!" she says, smiling. "This is Shane."

"Hey, don't you bartend at Lucky's?" Jacob asks, as they shake hands.

"Yep. That's me."

"Ah, I love that place. Well, nice meeting you here at my… office." He extends two hands outward in mock pride.

"How's the yak burger business?" Shane asks.

"Pretty good, man. Me and my cousin go to Alberta twice a year. Bring home some dead yak. Got a co-packer in Jamaica. Sell it here on weekends. Getting into retail markets as well. It's great."

"Are you still at Schecter and Wahl?" Zora asks.

"Nah, I do this full time," Jacob says. "Traded in my silk suit for these snazzy overalls." He runs a thumb under a faded denim shoulder strap.

"Really?" asks Zora.

"Yep. We just got into Trader Joe's. You wouldn't believe what city folk will pay for exotic game. You want to try?"

"Sure," says Shane. "We'll take two."

Jacob places two burgers on the grill. "Half price for you guys. That's sixteen."

"That's half?" Shane asks, with a raised eyebrow.

"Hey, it's New York," says Jacob. "And these are good."

Shane hands him a twenty. "Keep it," he says.

"Thanks, man," Jacob says.

Shane is suddenly struck with a slight pang of anger, its origins unclear. Something in the combination of Zora's excitement at seeing this guy, and his charging sixteen dollars for a hamburger, has him feeling territorial.

"I'm curious," Shane says, "how much does making one yak burger cost you?"

Zora looks at him, a bit taken aback, but Jacob answers as if asked where he bought his camo Converse high-tops.

"Well, I mean, if I bought the materials wholesale, maybe seventy, eighty cents. Then there's the bun. Another ten."

Shane's eyes widen.

"Wow," says Zora, "and you get sixteen bucks for them?"

"Well, you gotta remember. I don't buy wholesale, so it's a bit more complex. I have to travel to get the yak, transport it, keep it fresh, process it. That all adds up."

"To sixteen dollars?" asks Shane skeptically.

"Of course not," Jacob says. "Maybe six."

Shane scowls, suddenly regretting having to wait around this guy for the burgers to be cooked.

"Wow," he says, shaking his head.

"You disapprove," Jacob says, smiling.

Why is this lumberjackoff smiling? Shane thinks. He's tempted to leave his two burgers and twenty bucks and split.

"Kinda," he says. "I mean, ten dollars is a hell of a markup on a hamburger."

"Ah, but it's not a hamburger. It's a YAK burger!" Jacob says, proudly flipping the burgers in a flourish of flames and capitalism. "Hamburgers have been around forever. They're boring. Yak is new, it's exciting, it's—"

"Trendy," Shane says, disgusted.

"Yes!" Jacob says, with an enduring confidence and pride that makes Shane want to punch him. "The same reason you probably have a three thousand dollar Mac instead of an eight hundred dollar PC, Nikes instead of Keds, and drink eight-dollar IPAs instead of four-dollar Buds." Jacob presses the burgers onto the grill, releasing an aromatic cloud of yak smoke.

The heat rising in his cheeks, Shane looks down at his $100 sneakers and considers his MacBook Air and disdain for domestic beer.

"And people are free to tell me to take my overpriced yak burgers and stick 'em up my butt, but they don't. They keep buying them for sixteen dollars. They want more and more. The artisan food business is just like every other business; the price of something is determined by what people will pay for it. Applies to everything. Jeans, BMWs, computers… and yak burgers." He slides the burgers off the grill onto two waiting buns, places them on paper plates, and hands them to Shane and Zora with a wide, not unfriendly grin. "Enjoy."

Shane grabs the plates and warms up a little. As much as he disagrees with everything Jacob is saying, he can't help it, and he hates himself for thinking it; he doesn't know how it was possible, but this bearded Barnum was, well… cool. Likable. Shane and Zora each take a bite.

"Okay," Shane finally says. "I'm not sure I agree with, well, anything you're saying, but these are good."

"Thanks," says Jacob. "Try the Moosetard. We make that too. It rocks."

"Mmm, really good," Zora says, chewing happily. "So this is your full-time gig now?"

"Yup."

"You dig it?" asks Shane, squeezing some yellow Moosetard onto his burger, still not quite on board with Team Jacob.

"Let's just say I can't even imagine going back to an office job. Money aside, this isn't a job, it's my life, and I get paid to live it. It's great."

"You really should sell that salad stuff here," Zora says to Shane between bites.

"No," Shane says sharply, borderline offended by the suggestion. "I don't want…"

"You got something?" Jacob asks with wide-eyed curiosity. "I know the guy who runs this thing. He can get you a good spot."

"Thanks. No. It's just some stuff I make. Nothing worth selling here."

"Dude, you're eating a sixteen-dollar slab of yak ass. What is it?"

"It's just salad spritz."

"It's so good," Zora says.

"It's not," Shane says. "Well, I mean, it is, but, no, no one's going to buy it."

"Yak. Ass." Jacob repeats. "You're eating yak ass."

"Okay, okay," Shane says, unable to help laughing. "But I'm not… I'm not a businessman."

"Do I look like a businessman to you?" Jacob says, holding his arms out to reveal his flannel shirt, stained overalls, and Bee Gees mesh baseball cap.

"Well, no," Shane admits. "But you must have known business stuff before this?"

"Before this, I was an entry-level graphic designer at a giant marketing firm. I spent six years getting drafts of owls and rockets and shit rejected by people I never met."

"What did your parents do for a living?" Shane asks, trying to punch a hole in this guy's artisanal armor.

"Elementary school teachers."

"Really? Mine too. So where did you learn the food business?" Shane asks, with genuine curiosity.

"The Internet. And I just met a bunch of the right people and asked them a bunch of questions. Two?" he shouts to a couple waiting at his table. They nod.

"Yeesh," Shane grumbles. "Networking. I don't know if I can do that."

"It's only networking if you choose to call it that," Jacob says. "I think of it as hanging out. Making friends with common interests, talking, learning about them and from them, and making money along the way. It's just like socializing. With profits."

Shane looks at him and says dismissively, "I don't know if I can do that."

Jacob drops two sizzling yak burgers on the grill, and looks at Shane with a raised eyebrow through a cloud of smoke.

"Aren't you a bartender?" he asks.

A thoroughly-inked waitress drops off two Saturday afternoon beers for Shane and Zora, who are sitting at a cocktail table at a stylishly divey Williamsburg bar.

"Thanks," says Zora to the almost-smiling waitress. Shane is looking at his phone.

"Ha!" he says. "MeMeMe.com just tore that hedge fund guy who bought the Mets a new one. Found embarrassing old pics of him when he was twelve, dressed up as Mike Piazza."

"Whoa, what did he do?" Zora asks.

"Uh, nothing," Shane says, confused, looking at her over his phone. "I mean, just the Piazza pics. It's just funny.

He was such a fanboy that he bought the team. What a douche."

"Um, yeah," Zora says dryly. "Totally."

"Ha! Listen to this," Shane says, reading from the screen. "'When asked why he purchased the team he said, 'I wanted to. I can. So I did.'" Can you believe that?"

"No, I can't believe that that's… uh, in there," Zora says. "Hey, what do you think about what Jacob was talking about?"

"What? About what?" Shane says, taken aback by Zora's lack of interest, and the abrupt change of conversational trajectory.

"About his yak burgers. His business."

"What about it?"

"Are you considering it?"

"Yak burgers? No."

"No, you jerk," Zora says, laughing. "The salad stuff."

"What? No!" Shane yells. "Jeez, Zo, why do you keep asking me?"

"Sorry. I'm just trying to help."

"I don't need help, Zora. I'm fine."

"I know that. It's just, well, Jacob seemed so—"

"So, what?" Shane interrupts, his Jacob-fueled anger from earlier returning.

"Happy? Content? Alive? I don't know."

"I'm happy! And, I can't… I don't want to. A business owner? Me? No. I've never wanted that."

"I don't think Jacob did either," Zora says. "But I think he's glad he is one now."

"Nope. Not for me. I don't like the whole idea of selling and profiting from others. It's just slimy."

Zora takes a sip of beer, partly to put something in her mouth to stop what she really wants to say from coming out, and partly to deaden the pain of that all-too-familiar feeling she's gotten so often after meeting someone new. Disappointment.

When Zora's father left her and her mother to pursue his non-existent writing career, she was sad; but more than that, she was angry. She's since come to appreciate her dad for the one thing he was to her after his exit: an example of exactly what *not* to be. She looked at his high and mighty attitude, looking down on just about everyone while accomplishing nothing, a pathetic manifestation of all that is wrong with people. With his receding hairline and sad ponytail, which he actually dyed gray to make him appear more "distinguished," he was the epitome of someone who demanded respect and admiration but did nothing to earn it. He hated successful people. He regarded their success as an affront to *him*. He didn't understand why they didn't worship *him*. He hated businessmen, capitalism, and the entire idea of

America. Zora did not. She decides now that some things are worth fighting for, and fires the first shot.

"What about Henry?" she asks.

Shane, confused, says, "At the bar? What about him?"

"You like him, right?

"Yeah, of course, he's a good friend. And a good boss. Why?"

Zora had been indoctrinated during her youth into hating the wealthy and the successful, as her father blindly grouped them all into the same evil club. But after seeing him fail on the most basic level of human decency, she felt a de facto affinity for all things her father despised. Sixteen at the time of his leaving, she was already in full rebel mode, but his departure put her over the edge. She did the unthinkable. She typed her father's favorite phrase, "conservative assholes," into a search engine, and started reading.

"He's profiting from other people," Zora says to Shane. "He's a businessman."

"That's different. He's got a nice place. People enjoy themselves there. It's not some sleazy money-grabbing operation."

"Yours would be?"

"No! Of course not."

"Then what's the issue?"

"Zo, you heard Jacob. He makes those burgers for less than a dollar and sells them for sixteen! Does that seem fair to you? That's just greed. Capitalism at its worst."

Zora's Internet search had returned the usual suspects at the top of the list: Rush Limbaugh, Ann Coulter, and Bill O'Reilly. But she scrolled down a bit and found Walter Williams, David Horowitz, Thomas Sowell, Fredric Bastiat, and many more. While they certainly were conservative, as much as she read, she couldn't figure out the "asshole" part. Her anger at her father increased, and she hate-read the works of these men voraciously, learning things about economics, politics, and morality that she hadn't learned in school, and most definitely not from her father. Then for good measure, she read Mein Kampf and the Bible.

"Those people lined up at Smorgasburg didn't exactly look like *Forbes* subscribers," she says calmly. "And they all looked quite happy as well."

"Whatever, Zo, that's not the point. Whoever is buying something, for whatever reason, should know if they are paying like, nine hundred times what the thing they are buying is worth. Or it's fraud."

"How much is a screwdriver at the bar?" Zora asks.

"Seven bucks, why?"

"And how much do you guys get a bottle of vodka for?"

"Twel-"

The look of realization and defeat on Shane's face is acute and instant. He angrily sips his beer and looks down at his phone again. Zora feels the sharp pain of another self-inflicted slash from the double-edged sword one wields while enjoying the knowledge that comes with reason, research, and reflection—but still being alienated by a population that would just as soon not bother with any of these things. Once, when she was seventeen, one of her cousins—a fourth-year political science major at a forty-thousand dollar a year liberal arts college—started spouting about why the Electoral College should be eliminated, at a family barbeque. Zora politely proved in three sentences its necessary role in a representative republic and its vital role in insuring the stability of a nation of independent states. Her cousin walked away in a huff, saying, "Well, I didn't know you, well, like, knew stuff." The downside of "knowing stuff," as Zora learned long ago, is that it tends to piss people off. She'd learned to keep her opinions to herself. Usually.

Shane's festering anger migrates from Jacob to Zora. It moves up from his stomach to his cheeks, and then his ears. He doesn't know why Zora keeps wanting to talk about his stupid salad spritz, and financial stuff, but he doesn't like how it's making him feel about her. He looks up from his phone.

"What the fuck, Zora? I don't need this. Why are you pushing me to do something I keep saying I don't want to do?"

"I'm sorry," she says, taking his hand. *Baby steps, Zora, she reminds herself. He's a good guy. He hasn't had to adult all that much yet. Don't scare the shit out of him, for God's sake.*

"Really," she continues. "I'm not pushing you to do anything. It's just that it seems you have some pre-conceived notions about being a businessman, entrepreneur, capitalist, etc., that are just wrong. Don't sell your stuff, I don't care. Just don't miss a great opportunity because you have bad information in your head."

Shane takes a sip of beer and stews silently. What the hell was this girl talking about? How on Earth did he wind up sitting in a bar in Williamsburg with a girl he *thought* was cool, listening to her go on and on about the merits of capitalism? Capitalism was everything fucked up with the country and the world, and everyone knew that. Well, everyone except maybe Sam, and now apparently Zora as well. As far as Shane was concerned, politics and economics were two things that never really needed to be discussed or thought about, assuming you weren't greedy or power hungry. Especially with someone you were dating. Why didn't people understand how simple it really was? Don't be greedy. Be nice to each other. If everyone would just live by those simple rules, there wouldn't need to be all this talk about politics and economics. And if anyone doesn't follow the rules, that's what the government's for, to make sure people are nice and not greedy. Simple.

Shane didn't understand how his so-called "friends" didn't realize this, and frankly, how the government continually seemed to screw up their incredibly simple job. What perplexed him more than all this, however, was why in the hell, as he sat there fuming, looking into Zora's eyes, he didn't want to get away from her. He wanted to be with her. What she was saying was batshit crazy, but she certainly didn't seem to be. As much as she was pissing him off, he felt the uncontrollable urge to stay. She seemed to genuinely care for his well-being in a way he had never encountered before, even while she spewed all this BS about business and sales and stuff, kind of talking to him like a child. She was challenging his happiness. He didn't like that. But for some reason, he couldn't help but want to listen to her. To hear what weird stuff would come out of this seemingly sane girl's mouth next. He gives her hand a squeeze.

"Can we talk about something else? Please?" he asks.

"Sure," she says. "Like what?"

"Um, what book are you reading?"

"Jonathan Livingston Seagull."

"What's it about?" Shane asks, a bit mockingly. "A bird?"

"No. Not really. You should read it," she says, then after a moment, smiles at him and says, "Maybe not today though."

"Okay," Shane says, intrigued and confused. He's certainly never met a girl like this one before.

"How'd we do?" Shane asks.

"Eh, fine. Mondays are always slow after football season," Henry says.

Shane is finishing up his shift at Lucky's, wiping down the bar and saying good night to the last customers as they stumble merrily out the door. Henry, the owner, is at the bar register, reconciling the night's receipts while munching on a salad.

"Might have to raise drink prices a bit, the electric bills are killing me," he says. "Anyway, we can get home before three. Maybe shtup the wife, ya know?"

"That's… uh, that's fantastic, Henry," Shane says, not looking up from the bar he's wiping down.

"Who am I kidding?" Henry says. "The kid and the dog will be in my bed sandwiching my wife, and I'll be on the couch as usual. Hey, who's that little scooter I've seen you with?"

"Zora?" Shane asks. "She's cool, yeah."

"You hitting that?"

"Jesus, Henry."

"Sorry… I mean, I wish you two all the very best."

"Yeah, thanks," Shane says, rolling his eyes.

"Send me video. Hey, what's this I hear about you and your magic salad dressing?"

Shane scowls. "Oh jeez, really?"

"What's the matter? Couple of people said you make a mean salad whiz or something."

"Spritz. I make it once in a while. Just a hobby. That's all."

"Want me to buy some for the bar?"

"Sure, I'll bring in a bottle," Shane says, making a note in his phone.

"I was thinking ten," Henry says, while committing a masticatory hate crime on an artichoke heart. "Have any here? Let me taste some."

Shane shrugs, grabs a spray bottle, and hits Henry's salad. He gives it a try.

"Ten bottles might be tough," Shane says. "I'd have to see what they have at the markets, and-"

"Cases," Henry says, happily munching. "Gimme ten cases."

"Ten cases?!" Shane yells in disbelief. "Like, one hundred and twenty bottles? I don't think so."

"Sweet baby Jesus, that's good," Henry says, looking at the salad like it's a lingerie model.

"Thanks. Apparently it's good on pasta too."

Henry looks up from his salad for a moment, puts his fork down, pulls a bar stool over and sits down. "Listen," he says, "James took that sous chef gig at the Marriot."

"Shit," says Shane.

"With Ivan running the kitchen, I'm gonna need all the help I can get. So how about it?"

"Henry, I'd love to help, but you aren't listening," Shane says, tossing the bar rag in a bucket. "I don't have a business set up to crank out cases of the stuff. It's just me in my kitchen in Bushwick."

"No, you aren't listening," Henry says. "I just offered to pay you to make a product for me. A lot of it. That's how businesses start. How much does it cost you to make a bottle?"

"One bottle?" Shane thinks. "I don't know. Maybe a buck."

"I'll give you five bucks a bottle."

Shane thinks for a moment and looks at Henry, slightly perplexed.

"Why would you do that?" he asks warily.

"Buy a great product from a good friend and kick-ass worker who's made me a lot of money over the years, and his product will make me even more? Why wouldn't I?" Henry grabs his fork and takes another bite. "Fuck my sister, that's good."

"Henry. Thanks. But come on. I don't have anything in place to make a batch of the stuff. I don't have ingredients, room, a licen…"

"Five thousand," Henry says, annihilating a baby carrot.

"Excuse me?" Shane asks, shocked and confused.

"Would five thousand bucks help you get started?"

"Started with what? There's nothing starting here!" Shane insists. "Henry. Come on. Be serious."

"I am. Serious as the Pope on a Sunday. I'll give you five grand to help you get started. I'll get you going, and then if you ever make a profit, and by the taste of this stuff, I'm betting you will, I'll take five percent. I'll have my lawyer draw up a simple agreement. If you want a lawyer to look at it, I'll pay for that too. That's probably not legal, so don't tell anyone about that part."

Shane is hearing what Henry is saying, but experiencing it like a fever dream. *This is not right,* he thinks. *This is not how things are supposed to happen.* He couldn't just take five thousand dollars from his friend to make some stupid salad topping. He wasn't sure what had gotten into Henry, but he wasn't going to be a part of it.

"Henry. No. This is, I mean, thanks, but no. I don't know anything about the food business. And I don't know if this stuff will even sell."

"Well, you already have one commercial client."

"Who?" Shane asks.

"Me, you dumbass!" Henry bellows. "Are you paying attention?"

"Yes. Okay, fine. But… but, if I can't make the five thousand to pay you back, I don't have it. I can't. I can't do it."

"Shane," Henry says, reaching full exasperated-dad level. "Is that fucking man-bun cutting off the blood to your brain? I did not say I will *loan* you five thousand dollars. I said I will *give* you five thousand dollars to start your salad jizz business. It's a risk *I'm* taking. On you. You don't owe me shit unless you profit. Now, what do you say?"

"Spritz," Shane says quietly. After a moment, he says, "You are just going to trust me with your five thousand dollars?"

"Well, I mean, I know where you live, and I have some boys in Jersey," Henry says with a smile. "I'm kidding. Listen. I know trust is a strange, foreign concept these days, but just about every business, from Apple, to Sony, to Facebook, started with someone trusting someone with their money. That's how it happens. I got 10k from my mother-in-law to open this place."

"And you paid her back?" Shane asks.

"Yes," Henry says. "By feeding and housing her daughter and granddaughter. Business isn't always a straight-up cash transaction. But in this case, I'm quite confident by the fucking paranoia you are displaying right now that you aren't going to go out and buy a motorcycle or pile of blow with my money. So do you want it or not?"

Shane shakes his head, thinking. He knew he didn't want to get involved in any of what Henry was talking about, and he really didn't want to have this conversation any longer. It was making his head hurt.

"I don't even have a name," he says, fumbling over excuses in his mind. "For the spritz… the business…"

Henry shakes his head, rummages around in a pile of supplies behind the bar register, and pulls out a business check binder. "What's the main ingredient?"

"Uh, ramps?" Shane says.

"What the fuck is a ramp?"

"An aromatic vegetable. Kind of like a scallion."

Henry scowls and starts writing in the binder. "Okay, I see you need some motivation," he says. "So, I'm writing this check to your new company that doesn't exactly exist yet. I took the liberty of naming it. Now, all you need to do is go to city hall, file for a DBA, open a bank account, and deposit this check in it. Then start buying ramspit scallion stuff, and fill my order."

Henry rips the check out of the binder and hands it to Shane. It's a five-thousand-dollar check written out to "Citizen Shane's Ramp Spritz, Inc."

"Six hundred of that's for my first order," Henry says, holding out his hand. "Deal?"

Shane stares at his hand. He doesn't like being pushed, especially into opening a business, but he's oddly touched by Henry's kindness and confidence in him. And he's run out of reasons to turn him down. "I don't know what to say," he finally says.

"You should say, 'Who's there?'" says Henry.

"Why?" asks Shane.

"'Cuz opportunity just knocked on your door, my friend."

CHAPTER 4

"Whoa," says Gio, blowing out a cloud of smoke.

Shane, Gio, and Sam are sitting on the floor of Shane's living room, staring at his coffee table and smoking a joint. The object of their attention, lying on the coffee table, is the five-thousand-dollar check.

"I know," says Shane.

"That is so sexy," says Sam.

"I know," says Shane, picking up the check.

"That says five thousand, doesn't it?" Gio asks, passing the joint to Sam.

"Yep," says Shane.

"Dude," says Sam, exhaling. "Let's go cash it."

"Well, slow down there now," says Shane. "First off, I can't. Look who it's written out to."

Sam looks curiously at the check and passes the joint to Shane.

"Citizen Shane's… what the fuck is that?" he asks.

"The name of my company, apparently," Shane says, passing the joint to Gio.

"You don't have a company," Gio says.

"That's why I can't cash it," Shane says. "Besides, I don't know if I'm going to."

Hearing this, Gio almost burns his face off, fumbling and dropping the joint. Sam stares at Shane.

"I'm sorry," he says coldly, "I thought I just heard you say you were not going to cash a five-thousand-dollar check someone gave you."

"Yeah. I thought I heard that too," says Gio, accusingly.

"You gotta understand, guys," Shane explains. "I can't just cash this and go buy beers and weed with it. If I cash it, I gotta start a business. How the hell am I supposed to do that?!"

"With five thousand dollars and your current boss signed on as your first customer! How could you screw it up?!" Sam yells and stands up. "Are you nuts?"

"He could be my only customer, ever," Shane says. "That ain't gonna pay the rent."

"That's a good point, I hear you," Gio says, as Sam shoots him a look of disbelief. "And what about culinary school?"

"Fuck culinary school!" Sam shouts. "You can sell this stuff to all the schmucks who went there without you!"

Gio looks up and passes Sam the joint. Sam grabs it and takes an angry hit.

"I don't know," says Shane. "I don't think I'm gonna do it. I just… I make enough money at the bar. Things are good with Zora. I don't think I can deal right now."

"This is fucked, man," says Sam, pacing angrily with the joint clenched in his fingers. "What do you need, a neon fucking sign that says, 'Once In a Lifetime Opportunity' flashing over your head?! If I had five thousand bucks I would invest in Sean's Apps and let it ride till I could buy my own island. I can't believe someone just offered that to you and you're going to pass. That's seriously fucked up."

Shane stares at Sam with a look of confusion, sadness, and guilt.

"Whoa, dude. Chill," Gio says.

"I'm sorry," Sam says, tossing the joint onto the table in frustration, "but I wake up every morning hoping someone with cash to invest will trust me enough to partner up. Never happens. I fucking dream of meeting some rich dude looking for an investment opportunity I can help him with. Now here we are, my dreams actually coming to life, in *your* life, and you are going to turn it down!? I mean, I can't even deal with you right now."

"Well, I'm sorry you feel that way, man," Shane snaps back. "I didn't think this would piss you off. Honestly, while thinking this all over, I wasn't even thinking about you. Thanks for reminding me that this is actually about you."

"Well, that's the problem," Sam answers angrily. "You're short-sighted. And selfish."

"Selfish!?" Shane yells, wide-eyed.

"Yeah, that's right," Sam says. "Selfish. You have an opportunity to succeed. Prosper. Thrive. Provide, employ, improve lives beyond your own. And you're passing it up. Why? Because you can't deal? Because you're happy? Of course you're happy, you idiot. You're a bartender! But you know the shitty thing about being a bartender? Eventually, you turn thirty!"

"That actually is a good point, yeah," Gio mumbles.

"And," Sam continues, "Good luck working for a guy who now thinks you're a moron for not taking his five thousand dollars!"

Sam storms out of the apartment and slams the door behind him. Gio and Shane look at each other, then at the check, then at the joint. Shane shrugs and picks it up. He tries to take a hit, but in the time that has elapsed, the spark has gone out.

"Shit," he says.

"Damn, that was good," Shane says. "You like?"

Later that night, Shane and Zora are snuggled up on his couch, watching the end credits of a movie beginning to roll on the TV screen.

"I can only get so into superheroes fighting monsters," Zora says.

"That wasn't a monster," Shane replies. "That was Dr. Scandalor after he figured out the genetic coding map of the ETUSDOF."

"Eat us what?"

"The ETUSDOF. The Earth Trust's Ultimate Soldier DNA Optimization Formula."

"Oh," Zora says. "I thought it was a monster. I like it even less now."

"Fine," Shane says, and clicks off the TV with the remote. "Next Monday is ladies' choice."

"Excellent," says Zora, smiling. "I love Monday movie night."

"I love you, too," Shane says, and instantly stops moving. And breathing. He's pretty sure his heart has stopped beating. He feels the heat rising in his face and sweat forming on his brow as he realizes what he said. Words start falling out of his face.

"I mean, it… them… shit." He gets up and starts straightening up things in his apartment that are already exactly where they're supposed to be. Zora looks at him calmly and smiles.

"You gonna be okay?" she asks.

"Yes," he says. "Sorry."

"It's okay," she says. "I don't love you either."

Shane looks at her, both relieved and disappointed.

"Yet," she adds.

Shane smiles. Zora gets up and puts her arms around him.

"Thought you were going to have a stroke there for a sec," she says, and gives him a kiss.

"Wanna go to bed?" Shane asks.

"It's early," Zora says.

"Well, we don't have to… sleep."

They giggle and kiss, until Zora pulls back a little.

"What?" Shane asks.

"Nothing," Zora says. "It might… I feel a little… it just not be a good time."

"Oh," says Shane. "Got it."

"Sorry. Let's sit down."

They settle in on the couch. "What's going on with you?" Zora asks. "Everything okay at Lucky's?"

"Oh. Yeah. All good," Shane says. "Oh, get this. Henry wants to invest in the salad stuff."

"Really?!" Zora lights up. "That's great! Right?"

"Yeah," Shane says, hesitantly. "I mean, it's great that he believes in it, and me, but I'm not taking him up on it. I'm giving him his money back."

Zora tries to contain her disappointment. This boy is so close to being a man. She really hopes he'll hurry up and get there. She likes him.

"He already gave you the money?"

"Yeah. Five thousand."

Zora looks a bit shocked. She lets her arms fall to her sides. "And you are going to give it back?" she asks.

"Zo, I told you. I like making the stuff, but I don't want to run a salad dressing business. I'm not a businessman. I don't like the whole idea of selling stuff, profit, running a business."

Zora proceeds forward cautiously. "Shane, you know at the agency, we meet with writers every day who spend their entire careers waiting for someone to believe in them enough to write a check. Some have twenty years of work trapped in their computers, waiting for that one person to believe in them, and set them free."

"That's different," Shane says. "That's their dream. This isn't my dream."

Zora says in a calm but firm voice, "I hear you, Shane, but I guess what I'm wondering is, what do you want? What are your dreams?"

"I don't know," Shane answers, looking around the room, as if his dreams and the answer to Zora's question may be in there somewhere. "Do I need to have dreams? I mean, I'm happy. Usually. Isn't that enough?"

"Yes. Maybe goals is a better word," Zora says. "Have any of those?"

Shane gets the feeling that is becoming all too familiar in his conversations with Zora. He hasn't felt it often in his life, and he's not exactly sure how to identify it, but he's pretty sure what he's feeling is, offended. Offended and uncomfortable with these repeated inquisitions about his adult responsibility, or lack thereof. He's about had it. He likes Zora, but he knows that there are plenty of fish in the ocean, and he's got many years of casting his line ahead of him. He's getting the urge to move on to a new pond, and he fires up the outboard.

"Well, what are your big goals there, Miss 'Lean-In?'" he snaps.

Without missing a beat, Zora replies, "Well, I'd like to be a junior agent within the year. Then a full agent within five. Then, if other agencies aren't courting me soon after, I'll look into becoming a partner, and if that doesn't happen, I'll start my own agency. Either way, I intend to be running an agency in the next ten years."

Shane stares at her, silent. He's definitely starting to think that he and Zora may have less in common than they might have thought. Who has their next ten years planned out? He doesn't know what he's doing *tomorrow*.

"But in the more immediate future," Zora says, "I have to pee."

She grabs her purse, heads into the adjoining bathroom, and closes the door most of the way. "I'm listening," she says.

Shane is not sure if he's more taken aback by Zora's clearly thought-out future or her brazenly girlfriend-like bathroom behavior. Some girls he's dated would have been crying by this point in the discussion. This one is casually peeing in his bathroom, waiting to hear about his hopes and dreams. He sits down on the couch, angry, perplexed, and a little intrigued.

"Well, okay," he says, thinking, annoyed with Zora and humanity in general. "Fine. Urghh, I'm twenty-seven. Twenty-seven is a crazy age. I swear, when I had conversations like this last year, everyone said stuff like 'You're only twenty-six, you're a kid, don't worry about anything, just enjoy yourself! You've got all the time in the world.' Then, my twenty-seventh birthday happens, and suddenly everyone's like 'Dude, you aren't a kid anymore, get your shit together!' What the hell is that? Suddenly I need goals and a life plan?"

"It's called growing up," Zora says calmly from the bathroom. "It's not always fun, and it doesn't always happen when you think it will."

"Well, I'd like to retain some control of my extended immaturity, if that's okay with everyone. I'm not interested in becoming the Spritz King of New York right now. Maybe when I'm older. When I have actual responsibilities. You want a goal? There's one, to avoid having actual responsibilities for as long as humanly possible. How's that?"

After a moment, Zora says from the bathroom, "Sometimes you can make those kinds of decisions. Sometimes, it's just not up to you." She comes out and smiles sweetly at Shane.

Shane, still flummoxed, says, "What's that supposed to mean?"

Zora holds up a pregnancy test stick. There is a big red plus sign on it. Shane stares at it. For a long time. He looks at Zora. Her expression is a reflection of his—joy, sadness, wonder, and confusion.

"Can I say 'Oh shit'?" Shane finally asks. "I know that's probably not the most chivalrous response in this situation but I really can't think of anythi-"

"Yes," she interrupts.

"Oh shit."

"Now can I have a hug please?" she asks, holding out her hands, her eyes beginning to water.

Shane gets up and gives her a big hug. He holds her for a long time; partly to avoid the impending conversation, partly to shield her from the fear in his eyes, and partly because he has no idea what to do next.

CHAPTER 5

"That's all, Mr. Foster," the clerk says, stamping a final document. "You are officially a business owner."

Inside the city clerk's office in Lower Manhattan, Shane takes the small packet of papers from her hand, making him the legal owner of the Corporation "Citizen Shane's Ramp Spritz, Inc."

"Jesus," Shane says, overwhelmed by all the adulting he has been burdened with lately. A strong hand grabs his shoulder and pats him reassuringly.

"Relax. It's all good," says Jacob, the yak burger purveyor, smiling and holding out his hand. "Congratulations. Welcome to the club."

Shane extends his hand, and they shake. Then he collects his papers, and they leave the clerk's office and head to the lobby of the government building.

"Thanks so much for coming and helping me get this set up," Shane says to Jacob. "I'll pay you back someday, when I can. At least I owe you a drink. Let me know when."

"How 'bout now?" Jacob asks.

Shane looks at his watch. "It's eleven thirty," he says.

"One great perk of owning your own business," Jacob says with a big bearded smile, "Day beers."

"But don't you have to work?"

"Sure. I do. When I have to. And this is a business meeting. Sort of."

"Okay, well, if you have to go, I totally understand."

"Lemme check with the boss," Jacob says, and pulls out his phone. "Oh wait," he says, putting his phone away, "that's me. Yep, I'm free."

Shane smiles and shakes his head.

Shane and Jacob clink glasses and each take a sip. They are the only patrons at a Wall Street Irish bar.

"Cheers," says Jacob. "And hey, congrats again. On the business, and the baby."

"Yeah. Cheers. And thanks," Shane says, a bit dazed. "Now what the fuck do I do?"

"Well, I can't help with the baby, although this should help pay for diapers."

"Last week I was a bartender," Shane says as he takes a large swig. "This week I'm a businessman who's about to be a father."

"Life gets overwhelming," Jacob says. "Just follow your heart. You'll be fine."

"Follow my heart?" Shane asks, slightly confounded. "I'm not auditioning for Broadway. I'm selling salad spritz."

Jacob takes a big sip of beer, a bit of foam nesting into his thick brown beard. He wipes it with a cocktail napkin.

"That was a big misconception I had when I got started in all this. I never thought of running a business as a 'passion.' Not something you 'put your heart into,'" he says, air-quoting as he goes. "That was for people who had 'talent.' And I'd always considered talent 'the ability to entertain people.' That's just wrong. You can have talent and passion for your business. In fact, to be good, you have to. Those in business who look at themselves as having a 'job,' and then at people on TV or in the movies as having talent and passion, short-change themselves and are not going to succeed."

"Interesting," Shane says. "I never thought of it that way."

"I get a rush when I close a big order with a new market," Jacob says. "I've never been on Broadway, but I bet it's the same kind of feeling. I just don't have an audience watching when I turn in a virtuoso performance."

"But business is a lot of numbers, laws, spreadsheets, suits, meetings," Shane scoffs. "Ugh."

"In the same way that rock and roll is about acoustical engineering and electronic circuitry. You think AC/DC is thinking about electromagnetic impulses when they crank into 'Whole Lotta Rosie' on stage?"

Shane laughs. "No," he says.

"That stuff gets taken care of when money is being made. Don't get bogged down in it. Don't ignore it, but don't let it stifle your passion. Passion for your product, that's *your* job. Follow your heart, but use your brain. You'll be fine."

"This is going to sound weird," Shane says, taking another sip. "I don't *feel* like a businessman."

"Good. Me neither. Honestly, I think most business owners would say the same. It's a perception thing. We don't feel like we think we are *supposed* to feel, from what we've learned in the papers, and in movies, books, and TV. But what is that feeling? Boring, greedy guy in a suit? How do you feel like that? That's not what we are. That's not real."

Shane nods, and thinks for a moment. "I don't even know what I don't know," he says. "Ugh."

"Let me ask you something," Jacob says. "Actually, picture something for me, okay?"

"Okay," Shane says.

"Alright. One year from now, there are millions of people around the world enjoying your salad stuff, on leftover pasta in their London flats, on Nicoise salad in French bistros, and on iceberg wedges and tomatoes at Texas family barbecues. You got that in your head?"

"Sure."

"Good. You *are* a businessman," Jacob says, sipping his beer. "And a good one."

"What?" Shane asks, confused. "How—"

"Because you're smiling."

Shane realizes that he is. He bows his head and holds up his glass, in pseudo-mock honor, to Jacob.

"That means you have the two most important things to make it in this business, any business: passion and vision," Jacob says. "Not everyone has that. A lot of businesspeople just want a yacht. They usually fail."

"I definitely don't want a yacht," Shane says.

"If you do someday, it's okay," Jacob says. "Buy one. Buy two. You will have earned it. The secret is to not let the cool stuff you buy guide your passions. Let your passions guide your business. Be passionate about your product." He finishes his beer.

"Copy that," Shane says. "I'm taking this all in. Thanks again for your help. I don't want to keep you. You must have… yak stuff to do."

"Any time, man. I mean it. You have my cell number. And my email. Hit me with whatever."

"Thanks. But…"

"But what?"

"I just, I don't want to take advantage," Shane says hesitantly. "I mean, you started your thing on your own. I'll figure it out."

"Hey, listen, there are no rules that say you have to do this on your own, you know," Jacob says. "That's not cheating. You'll learn all about that come tax time."

"Ha. Okay," Shane says, and finishes his beer. "I'm getting another. Want another?"

"Absolutely."

Shane flags down a waitress. "Two more IPAs," he says as she nods and heads to the taps.

"Can I tell you a story?" Jacob asks.

"Sure."

"I had a neighbor in the East Village in the late '90s, Orly. Hey, do you know what the '90s are?"

"Ha, fuck off, old man," Shane says. "How old are you anyway?"

"Thirty-five," Jacob says.

"Damn. You look young. Must be the beard."

"No. It's the business," Jacob says, smiling. "Anyway, Orly and I both had shit studios in the same shit building. Our dogs hit it off, we hit it off… He was a quiet kid, kinda shy, I think everyone thought he was flaky and stuck up, because he wanted to be an actor, and he was blond and good looking. But he was a cool guy. We became good friends."

The waitress drops off two fresh beers.

"Uh, okay," says Shane. "Was there a point?"

"Yes, grasshopper, pay attention," Jacob says with a smile as he lifts his beer mug.

"Grasshopper?" Shane asks.

"Forget it," Jacob says. "The point is, another thing to remember about being a successful businessman—you meet lots of people. Be nice to all of them." He takes a sip.

"Well, I generally am," Shane says. "Which is why I don't want to take advantage of you—"

"Be nice to everyone," Jacob interrupts, "because you never know when your shy, impoverished East Village slum-mate is going to grow up to become Orlando Bloom."

Shane stops drinking mid-sip and looks at Jacob with wide eyes.

"Orlando Bloom?!" he says. "The elf in the Hobbit movies?!"

"And the pirate in the Pirate flicks," Jacob says. "He's a ten *billion* dollar man at the box office."

"Holy shit," Shane says. "You keep in touch?"

"Yeah, sure. Not like we used to. He's in LA turning down supermodel proposals now."

"Wow, that's kinda awesome," Shane says, taking it all in. "Not sure what this has to do with your business, though."

"When Orly heard that I was thinking about leaving graphic design and starting up a business a few years ago," Jacob explains, "he put in twenty grand. He's a five percent partner in Yak, Inc."

"Ha! No way," Shane says.

"Yep. I send him a check every quarter. I don't think he would notice if I didn't… one didn't get cashed for nine months. Anyway, my point is, I wasn't alone either. I had help. Orly hooked me up with a lawyer too. I can do that for you. Passion, vision, good friends, and a big pile of luck are all factors in launching a successful business."

"Wow. Okay," Shane says. "But I still don't want to take up your time. I'm going to need so much help if I'm actually going to make this happen. I'm not sure what to do."

Jacob sees the worried look on Shane's face. One defective condom spun this kid's life one-hundred-eighty degrees. He looks into Shane's desperate eyes and feels bad. Then, he looks deeper and sees something more. Opportunity.

"Would you consider a partnership?" he asks.

"Wha—like… what?" Shane asks, surprised. "I don't even know what that would entail."

"Well, think about it," Jacob says. "You've got your recipe and your knowledge of the product, I've got the business experience. Might be a win-win."

"But, I couldn't like, pay you or anything," Shane says meekly.

Jacob smiles and takes a sip of beer.

"You really have to lose the worker-bee mentality," he says. "It's business. A new game. Your game."

"I guess I still don't know the rules," Shane says, and shrugs.

"You said Henry put in five thousand?" Jacob asks. "And he's getting five percent?"

"Yes. That's right," Shane says. "But he's got a family and a bar to run, so I don't think he wants to be heavily involved in helping me make this happen."

"So he's a silent partner," Jacob says.

"I guess so, yeah," Shane says.

"Well, I could be a louder one, if you will. Be involved every step of the way. For, say, twenty percent."

Shane looks at him, confused and hesitant.

"I can't give you twenty percent of Henry's investment," he says, smiling uncomfortably, fidgeting with a cocktail napkin.

Jacob gives Shane his best "disappointed dad" look.

"Another thing you should learn about businesspeople and business deals. Not everyone is trying to fuck everyone. Some certainly are, but only in books and movies is it a full-on gladiatorial battle of greed. I'm not asking for any money. I'm offering ten thousand for a twenty percent stake."

"What?! No. No way! I can't. This is getting crazy."

Jacob reaches over and pats Shane on the arm, trying to console him, but unable to help laughing a little.

"Calm down," he says. "Everything's fine. Breathe. Just think about it. My business is doing great. We're projecting a quarter-million dollar profit this year. It ain't *Lord of the Rings* money, but it's something. I can either give half of that to Uncle Sam to build shitty roads and schools with, or I can invest it. And I want to invest in your stupid salad spritz. Think about it. If you say no, I will still help you, even though that would be me just being nice, so you couldn't tell the other evil businessmen, or they won't let me come to the annual kitten-drowning party."

Jacob smiles. Shane thinks. Then he drinks. Then he holds out his hand.

"Fuck it," he says. "Let's do this."

They shake hands.

CHAPTER 6

"FUUUUUUUUCK YOOOOUUUUUUUUUUUU!"

Zora screams as she lies back on the delivery table, pushing at the behest of the doctors, nurses, and Shane. She's sweating and panting, trying unsuccessfully to remember the breathing exercises she learned in the birthing classes. Shane stands by her head, trying his best to be supportive. A doctor at the other end of the bed expertly wrestles her long blonde hair into a messy bun and gets ready to receive the baby.

"Okay, one big push, Zora," she says. "You're doing great."

"UUUUUNNNNNNGGGHHH!"

"Good job, Zo," Shane says. "I love you. Remember your breathing."

"Fuckyoufuckyoufuckyoufuckyou," Zora says in rhythm with her breathing.

Shane looks around, embarrassed. A nurse mouths the word "Drugs," crosses her eyes, and smiles sympathetically. Shane manages to smile back meekly.

"Okay," says the doctor. "I see the head."

"IS IT A FUCKING HIPPO HEAD?! CHRIST!"

"Doing great, sweetheart, doing great," Shane says, with as much empathy as he can muster. "I love you."

"I love you, too," Zora says. "I'm going to fucking kill you!"

"Okay, we'll talk about that later. Now, breathe… push…"

"UNGGHHHHHHHHRUUGGH!"

There is a moment of release and relief in the room, and then, the soft shrieks of a newborn baby fill the air.

"Oh," Zora gasps at the sound.

Shane's mouth drops open at the thought of an additional person having magically entered the room, and the world. The doctor holds up the squirmy, crying baby and brings it to Zora.

"Congratulations," she says. "Meet your daughter."

"Our daughter," Shane says, the words getting caught in emotion and awe.

Zora's focus moves instinctually from her own pain and trauma to that of her daughter. Almost desperately, she holds her hands out to take her.

"Oh," she says again, as she takes the tiny girl in her arms. Zora holds her close. "Hi, beautiful."

Shane touches Zora's hair and stares at the baby, mesmerized. "Oh my God," Shane says. "She's… she's… perfect."

Zora looks at Shane.

"Hope?" she says.

Shane nods.

"Hope," he says. "We love you, Hope." He kisses Zora on the cheek. "Please don't kill me," he says. "I don't want to miss this."

"I won't," Zora says.

CHAPTER 7

It's an especially busy Smorgasburg, with good weather bringing foodsters from the far reaches of New York City to partake in some of the region's finest artisanal cuisine. Shane is set up in a tent next to Jacob. There are dozens of bottles of professionally labelled "Citizen Shane's Salad Spritz" and "Citizen Shane's Pasta Spritz" displayed on a folding table in front of him.

These two "varieties" contain the exact same ingredients, despite Shane's objections. After seeing how much exchanging even a teaspoon of basil for a teaspoon of parsley would cost, not to mention the months-long bureaucratic tailspin it would send the FDA into, he abandoned this morally-dictated distinction and acquiesced. Jacob reminded him that business was all about compromise. Quality vs. cost. How low you can go before pissing off your customers. Your goal, he said, was to never find out.

The labels, though mass-produced at a massive print house in New Jersey, look like they were individually scribbled with Sharpie markers to make the product feel like it was made and bottled right in Shane's own kitchen, not a gigantic co-packer in Queens. Traditional bright whites and bold, clean vegetable colors have been forgone for an amber bottle and minimalist terra cotta and yellow label, antiqued and randomly jagged-edged as dictated by the industrial printers' label-making software. By intentional design, the product looks more like microbrewed beer in a spray bottle than salad dressing. Jacob reminded Shane that image is everything—from the shoes you wear, to the car you drive, to the labels on your salad spritz. His approach was simple; he wanted to do something that had never been attempted before. He wanted to make salad dressing cool.

There is a crudité-type spread for sampling on one of the tables in front of Shane, but no customers around to sample anything. Jacob, meanwhile, has a line of people waiting for yak burgers at his tent.

"How's baby girl?" he yells to Shane, between serving burgers.

"Oh, good," Shane says. "It's a full-time job just keeping her alive, but it's great. Zora's a good momma." Four people slow down as they approach his tent, then speed up to join the yak burger line. Shane yells to Jacob, "Hey, do you need a hand over there?"

"No, all good," he says. "You be ready over there. They'll come."

"You said that last week."

"Give it time. Took about two months until people developed a taste for yak parts. Patience, my friend. That's fifteen," he says to a customer, as he trades a burger for a twenty.

"Okay," Shane says, surveying the emptiness before him. "Hopefully something happens soon. Selling spritz to friends and family isn't gonna put Hope through college."

"She can work for me," Jacob says, white teeth flashing from amidst his beard.

"Haha," Shane says. "But seriously. I can't believe how much of the investment money is gone just from making one initial batch."

"Two batches!" Jacob says. "One salad, and one pasta."

"They just have different labels," Shane says brusquely.

"Shhh!" Jacob scolds. "Brilliant, I know. You're welcome. Thirty bucks, thanks!" he says to a customer. "Now all you gotta do is sell."

Shane looks at the vast span of no people at all in front of his tent.

"That would require having someone to sell *to*," he says to himself.

A distinctive voice cuts through the warm Brooklyn air.

"Jake, you lumbersexual WANKER!"

Shane turns to see the source of the shouting, and is amazed to see that it's none other than Orlando Bloom, standing next to Jacob's tent with a gorgeous girl who, if she isn't a famous model, should be. The crowd notices as well, and starts buzzing and squealing.

"Orly!" Jacob says. "What the hell? Good to see you. What are you doing here?"

"Charlotte's in a wedding in the city tomorrow. Thought I'd drop by and surprise you, you yak-slinging fool. Charlotte, Jacob."

"Nice meeting you," Jacob says, as they shake hands. "I have some stories for you."

"Oh really?" Charlotte says, bubbling with excitement.

"Don't even," Orlando says. "I know people in LA who know people. I'll have you killed."

"Ha. Hey, Orly, this is my buddy Shane," Jacob says, gesturing in Shane's direction with a spatula. "I just invested in his company."

"No shit? Hello, Shane," Orlando says, making his way over to Shane's tent with Charlotte in tow.

"Hi," Shane says as they all shake hands. "Really great to meet you."

The crowd has begun snapping pics of the scene. Shane is a little freaked out, while Orlando doesn't seem to notice.

"Likewise," he says, picking up a spritz bottle. "You know I got that yakfucker started, right?"

"I heard," Shane says, laughing. "I guess he's, uh, yakking it forward." Shane winces at his dumb, starstruck-induced joke, looks at Jacob for help, and gets a "Don't worry about it" head shake. Orlando doesn't seem to have even heard, being fully engrossed in a salad spritz bottle's label.

"What the fuck is a ramp?" he asks.

"It's an aromatic vegetable," says Shane. "Like a scallion."

"Right on," says Orlando.

"Dude, try some," says Jacob. "It's badass."

Orlando grabs a piece of celery, then a bottle, spritzes, and bites. He chews earnestly and takes another taste. With no indication to the positive or negative, he pulls out his phone.

"Mind if I take a pic?" he asks Shane.

"No," Shane says. "Course not."

"You gonna send that to your chef so he knows what to put in your trailer?" Jacob says. "You're not getting it in exchange for movie tickets there, big baller."

"Fuck off," Orlando says. Shane can't help smiling, watching his burger-flipping friend giving this movie megastar the business. Orlando places himself next to Shane's display bottles, grins, and takes a selfie. Then he starts typing on his phone, still chewing.

"How the fuck do you spell Smorgasburg?" he asks.

"S-M-O-R-G-A-S-B-U-R-G," Jacob says. Orlando continues typing.

"Aaaaaand hashtag. Good. Thanks," says Orlando.

Suddenly the crowd buzzes anew. Cell phones begin whirring and pinging and chirping all around. People look at them to see what's going on. Jacob and Shane do as well.

"Holy shit!" Shane says.

"And... boom," Jacob says quietly, checking his phone with one hand while deftly flipping a burger with the other.

On Shane's phone, a new Tweet reads

@BloomOrlando Tweeted: "Get your sweet arses to #Smorgasburg and buy some of this stuff now. It's awesome. I'm here! Cheers! #citizenshane #whatthefuckisaramp"

Shane looks up and sees a throng of hungry hipsters headed toward his tent.

"Oh shit, oh shit, oh shit," he says. "Orlando! Mr. Bloom! Thank you!"

"No worries, mate," Orlando says. "That stuff's fantastic. How much?"

"Nothing! Take all you want," he says, as the crowd descends on the tent. "Holy shit! Thanks."

"We'll ship you some," says Jacob.

"Right on, I'll have the people who know my address call your people!" Orlando says.

"Great!" Shane yells, wondering what it would be like to have "people."

A gaggle of girls cautiously approaches Orlando, vibrating with excitement.

"Orlando! Hi! Hi! Can we get a pic?" one asks.

"Of course, get in here, girls!" Orlando says. The girls gather around, passing their phones amongst each other, rushing to snap a few pics before Orlando vanishes in a cloud of stardust, as cooperative pop icons tend to do in these situations. Orlando finishes with the group of girls, strategically places himself in front of the spritz bottles for the next round, and gives Shane a wink. Shane gives him a thumbs-up and mouths "Thanks." The growing crowd begins snapping away. A line forms before Shane. Instead of reaching for their cameras, they are reaching for their wallets.

"Get ready," says Jacob, smiling. "It's about to get fun."

Shane smiles and breathes deeply. He considers the incongruity of Orlando Bloom and his might-as-well-be-a-supermodel girlfriend Charlotte posing in front of his spritz bottles in a city park in Brooklyn. He looks at Jacob, flipping yak burgers and smiling like a proud father at a barbeque watching his son learn how to dribble a basketball. He looks at the crowd in front of him, Orlando Bloom's electricity coursing through it, and his salad topping.

He thinks of Zora and his baby girl at home. They aren't going to believe this. His first thought is "this is stupid." His second thought is that after the birth of Hope, this is the most exciting moment of his entire life.

"How much?" the first person asks.

Shane stares for a moment, having forgotten the price.

"Eleven," he remembers proudly.

People start reaching for wallets and eagerly pulling out cash. He remembers the arguments he had with Jacob over the high price of the product, and is thankful he acquiesced. Shane starts trading bottles for bills as fast as he can. He gets into a rhythm, similar to the one he settles into behind the bar at Lucky's on a busy night. Orlando is passing out samples and people are jumping on the ever-growing line after they get a taste. Charlotte is goofily vamping and posing for pics as an impromptu "Spritz Bottle Model."

Shane is feeling something he didn't fathom he ever would as a business owner. Happy. Comfortable. Confident. And he hasn't even come close to turning a profit yet. He had always assumed that business was about doing unsavory and inherently unsatisfying things with your life, in exchange for the money that came with it. He's thankful he's figured out how to not be that kind of businessman. He's got something people really want, as evidenced by the massive line forming before him. He smiles with pride. He's selling bottles, one, two, three at a time.

"Eleven dollars. Thirty-three… that's eleven," he's saying to happy new spritz owners. "Eleven, twenty-two… shit. Jake! You have singles?"

Jacob looks in his cash drawer and shakes his head. He thinks for a moment, and yells to Shane's crowd, "Spritzmasburg Orlando Special! Two for twenty! Two for twenty!"

The crowd murmurs happily and starts holding out twenties while yelling, "Two! Two!" Shane looks at Jacob and they share a smile.

"I'll make up the difference!" yells Jacob.

"Don't be crazy!" Shane yells. "This is awesome! Thanks!"

Orlando slides in next to Shane, fist bumps him, and starts doling out spritz bottles to eager young Brooklynites.

"That's a good girl," Shane says to Hope later that night. "That's my girl."

As he puts baby Hope in her crib, she squirms and grunts, expressing readiness for bed in her own baby way. While Shane has always been generally happy to have Hope and Zora in his life, they were, for lack of a better term, a happy accident. Although the logical parts of his mind told him otherwise, a constant feeling remained that they were temporary. Not exactly real. Like a dream. Not one of those fantastic ones where you fly around your neighborhood naked or play professional baseball; but not a nightmare either. One of those weird ones that can only exist in the world adjacent to consciousness. Like one where you have to stay home from your job as an actuary because your pet ferret has herpes and is depressed. Weird. He always felt that at some point, he would wake up, ending the weirdness, and get back to his actual life.

Tonight was different. He felt somehow changed. Present. Important. He felt like an actual father, not an accidental one. A real adult man, not one who got there too soon, necessitated by an unforeseen occurrence. He was the protector of his home, and his family. He saw his future, and there were three people in it. It was a bright one. He saw it clearly, and smiled. He found himself no longer regarding his new family as being somehow unlucky, but lucky. Instead of feeling somewhat sorry for Zora and Hope, he now realized their good fortune. How fortunate they were, fortunate to have him. He still wasn't sure about this whole salad dressing business, but he suddenly had a newfound sense of purpose, and a sense that he could, and should, accomplish great things.

"Love you," Shane says, as he kisses Hope on the head. "Sweet dreams, my little angel."

Zora is stretching out on the living room couch. She turns on the baby monitor and places it on an end table. Shane joins her on the couch and takes her hand. He kisses her gently on the lips and cheeks.

"Hi," Zora says, a bit taken aback by the affection which has diminished of late amid spit-up and salad spritz.

"Sorry I got home later than I planned to," he says.

"That's all right," Zora says. "I can't believe you met Orlando Bloom. I'm so jealous."

"I know. It was nuts. You hear back about the maternity leave yet?" Shane asks.

"Oh, I don't want to talk about that now," she says. "You had such a great day."

"I know, but it's important. Trying to figure out the future, you know? Any news?"

"No," Zora says. She sighs and smiles a little. She's heard Shane reference the future before, but she's pretty sure this was the first time he's done so without putting the word "fucking" in front of it.

"Everyone keeps saying it's going to happen," she continues, "even though my employee status changed mysteriously last month, apparently causing the country's entire health care system to implode. Got another bill from the hospital today."

"How much?" Shane asks.

"Eight thousand."

"Jesus," Shane says. "What exactly did the insurance policy mean by 'full maternity coverage'?"

"No idea. Don't know how much babies cost. Never made one before. Now tell me more about today. Please?"

"I can't believe I sold out," Shane says. "Made two thousand dollars. Not bad."

"Not at all! Good job." She looks at Shane, trying to decipher the look in his eyes. "You okay? There's a lot going on."

"Yeah, I'm good," he says, smiling. "You okay? Hope's a full-time gig, right?"

"Yeah. But she's good. I love her."

"Me too. I think we are doing okay as parents?"

"No idea."

"Me neither. Hey, I'm getting a beer," he says, getting up and heading to the kitchen. "Want one?"

"Still breastfeeding," Zora says calmly.

"Shit. I keep forgetting. I'll get a water."

"Have a beer, Shane. You just can't kiss me."

Shane stops and looks at her, slightly confused.

"Kidding," Zora says, smiling, silently thankful that Hope has brain DNA from both Shane *and* her.

Shane returns with a beer for himself and a water for Zora. He takes a sip.

"God, that's good. I don't remember when I last drank a beer. Oh, so, Henry's being flexible around the business, and me not getting any sleep. He's bringing in a guy to help clean up at night. I don't know how long that will all last, though. I think he's more worried about me passing out mid-shift than anything else."

"Well, maybe you can quit bartending soon," Zora offers with a sly smile.

"Well," Shane says, "that would be nice, but I'll need to make two thousand dollars on days when Orlando Bloom *doesn't* show up as my marketing guy. I'll order some dinner. Thai good?"

"Anything that doesn't involve my cooking it," Zora says, leaning her head back on the couch cushions.

Shane grabs his phone to place the order. As he looks at the screen, he sees a new email. He clicks it open, reads it over.

"Holy shit," he says, standing up abruptly.

"What?" asks Zora.

"It's from Whole Foods," Shane says. "'Dear Mr. Foster, it was a pleasure meeting you and your partner last week. Your product seems to have found a life on the internet, and we would like to meet to discuss a nationwide rollout of "Citizen Shane's Ramp Spritz." Salad and Pasta varieties. Please let us know when it would be convenient to meet.'"

"Oh my God," Zora says, leaning forward, suddenly fully awake and unsure what to do with her hands.

"Wow," Shane says, looking at Zora blankly. After a moment, she gets up and gives him a big hug. Shane notices after a moment that she's crying.

"Zora," he says. "Hey. What's the matter? This is good. I think."

"I'm so proud of you," she says softly, and hugs him again.

"Okay, don't cry then," Shane says soothingly. "I don't know how much I'm going to get on the deal, I mean, I—"

"Hey," she interrupts, backing away a step and taking Shane's hands in hers. "I'm proud of you. That's all. You did something good. I'm happy."

"Oh, okay," Shane says, smiling. "Good. I love you."

"I love you, too," she says.

"I should call Jake. Find out what this all means," he says, starting to dial, then hesitating. "Oh shit. The Thai."

"Thai can wait," Zora says. "Call Jake."

Shane dials and waits.

"Jacob- hey… Yeah, totally fun day, Orlando's awesome. I can't thank you enough… yeah, uh- I think I have some good news… Whole Foods emailed. They want to talk. They said 'nationwide rollout.'"

Shane has to move the phone away from his ear to avoid the aural blast of glee emanating from the large, bearded man on the other end of the line. He looks at Zora, who giggles and puts her hand to her mouth.

"Uh huh," Shane says. "Right. Okay… Hmm… Okay. Okay. What? How much? Dollars? Okay. Really? Okay, thanks. Right. Of course, of course. Call you later."

Shane hits the end button, cutting off Jacob, mid-victory shriek. He stares at nothing for a few seconds, then looks at Zora, who is brimming with anticipation.

"I think we should order steak," he says.

CHAPTER 8

"The more I see, the less I know for sure."

-John Lennon

Shane is sitting in a chair in an unglamorous, but professional and efficient-looking, studio space. He's getting a small lavalier microphone clipped onto his shirt collar by an audio technician. An attractive young woman with a nose ring is patting make-up on his brow, while another is tousling his hair to imperfect perfection. Shane is about to be interviewed for the internet vlog MeMeMe. A small camera crew is setting up their gear in front of him. Shane is excited and a bit awestruck at the idea of being interviewed for one of his favorite social media channels. MeMeMe has millions of followers. It's the cool place to go for news and happenings, as presented with a tough, genuine attitude that he and the rest of his attention-span-deficient generation appreciates. When some corrupt millionaire or politician does something unsavory, MeMeMe doesn't hold back; it calls them out, often in hilarious ways. Shane appreciates getting the real story. MeMeMe presents news in a fresh way, that makes him realize that not everyone is an asshole, and those who are aren't going to get away with it forever. He is humbled and grateful that MeMeMe has asked him to come in for an interview.

"Thanks for coming by the studio today, Mr. Foster," says MeMeMe founder Bristol Hart, entering the room and settling in a chair opposite Shane. The hair, make-up and audio folks turn their attention immediately to her. Bristol is thirty-one. With red "White House" style hair and a body worked into ballet dancer shape, she exudes an air of elegant gravitas. No one can remember what propelled her to the top of the blogosphere: her looks, Ivy League degree, or the money and influence her dad garnered over decades on Wall Street. Bristol relishes the irony of coming from a wealthy family and making a name for herself as a champion of the downtrodden and disenfranchised; she specializes in hit pieces on the wealthy, exposing their lavish lifestyles and elaborate possessions to her audience's fascination and disgust. Even though she can personally afford the very best, she tries to dress down as much as possible to avoid accusations of hypocrisy, saving the Givenchy dresses and Louboutin shoes for special dinners and charity events her followers could never afford to attend. Her father certainly wasn't happy about her "career" choice, but he resigned himself to the fact that this was who his daughter was, and she was, to his chagrin, good at it, and passionate; so he kept the fund gates opened. The website was profitable, sort of, not that it mattered. Dad's money provided the safety net below, and the air of success above. There she was now, perched on high in her temple, and Shane Foster has been invited to the altar.

"Please, it's Shane," he answers. "Six months ago, I was a bartender."

"Well, things certainly have changed, haven't they?" Bristol says amicably.

"Well," Shane says carefully, "Things may have. But I haven't. I'm the same."

Bristol is half listening, half checking her look in a hand mirror.

"Okay, that's good," she says. "So, I'm going to ask you about how it feels to go from bartender to salad dressing mogul, almost overnight. How you were able to achieve what so many other local artisans haven't been able to. Everyone loves a good local Brooklyn-Boy-Makes-It-Big story."

Shane sort of zoned out after hearing the word "mogul," but manages to nod in vague agreement. "So, it's like an inspirational piece," he says. "Got it. It should be, because, believe me, if I can do this, anyone can."

"Well, I'm sure it takes a special kind of talent," Bristol says, smiling into the mirror and checking her teeth for lipstick.

"Well, I mean, I guess," Shane says. "But I'm glad to be here, because I think it's really important, what you do. And for people out there to realize that they can, you know, be successful, make money, run a business, and not be, you know, an asshole. Sorry."

"No worries," says Bristol, smiling. "I hear you loud and clear."

"I'm not one of those rich businessmen you're always tearing a new one. I mean, obviously. Right?"

"Mr. Fos- Shane," Bristol says, looking up from her mirror and flashing a camera-ready smile. "We only tear apart those who deserve it."

"Good," Shane says, smiling back. "That's what I figured."

"We are rolling," the cameraman says.

"Do I look okay?" Shane asks. "I got a new shirt for this."

He strikes a silly pose. "Pra-daa!" he says. "Four hundred bucks. Got it for forty at T.J. Maxx."

Bristol smiles. Her cameraman nods to her.

"Looks like we're just about ready," she says. "You look great. Very successful. Okay, here we go." She morphs seamlessly into hostess mode, her face becoming the one that Shane has watched and admired and maybe even had a bit of a crush on over the years. His heart is thumping like a South Beach dance club. The cameraman points to her.

"Shane Foster, it is a pleasure to meet you," she says.

"Likewise," Shane says. "I'm a big fan of the website."

"You're very kind. Now, first things first, the question on everyone's mind. What on earth is a ramp?"

Shane smiles widely.

"What do you mean you can't?!"

Jacob is practically yelling at Ben Edgar, a fifty-five-year-old man with reddish-gray hair under an unironic John Deere mesh baseball cap. He's sitting behind a desk in a small, wood-paneled office that doesn't appear to have been updated, or cleaned, since the '70s. Shane is sitting in a chair across from Ben, and Jacob is pacing behind him. The sounds of farm equipment hum outside the office walls.

"You could make a ton of money here!" Jacob continues.

"Believe me, guys," Ben says earnestly, nervously brushing at some dirt that has been on his overalls longer than Shane has been on Earth, "I would love to help you. I've already got half my farm dedicated to your ramps. They ain't easy to grow, you know… short spring season's all ya get. Even if I dedicated my entire property to ramp production, I wouldn't come close to meeting your guys' needs."

"Can you buy more land?" Shane asks. "You'll be able to afford it."

"Ain't that simple," says Ben. "This ain't the wild west. It's New Jersey. Everything is owned by somebody, or some company. I'd have to take over another farm, if anyone's even looking to sell. And the government red tape, you have no idea. Might take years. That ain't gon' help nobody."

Shane and Jacob are listening, processing the unfortunate news. Jacob stops pacing. When they came to their supplier's farm with the news of the Whole Foods deal, they thought it would result in a celebration, not a tremendous roadblock.

"I can't believe I'm saying no, but I really can't do it," Ben says. "It's a matter of square mileage. I ain't got enough."

Shane looks at Jacob. "What are we gonna do?" he asks.

"I have no idea. We'll figure it out," Jacob says, with no conviction whatsoever.

"Can I make a suggestion?" Ben says.

"Sure," says Jacob.

"I did some research, and I don't know what you think of this, but it seems the Philippines might be your answer."

Shane stiffens at the mention and opens his mouth to protest. Ben holds up his hand and continues.

"Now just hear me out," he says. "I feel bad about the situation and I'm trying to help you."

The firmness and guilt in Ben's voice reminded Shane of when his father used to ground him for staying out on his

BMX bike past dark, or getting a C in algebra. He let Ben continue.

"They're getting into the ramp game. You can get what you need. Cheap, too. Cheaper than from me. Even with overseas shipping."

"No," says Shane sternly, once Ben is finished. "No way. This is a locally grown product. That's its selling point."

"Well," Jacob says, thinking. "We're going to be selling in Whole Foods stores around the country. And maybe internationally. So 'local' doesn't really mean anything, technically."

"Yes, but 'technically' buyers assume that the stuff is made in America," Shane says. "I mean, that's why it's expensive. And good."

"Like cars used to be," Ben says wistfully, looking out the window at something, most likely the past.

"I'm not really sure people will care," Jacob says to Shane. "It's still 'Citizen Shane's Ramp Spritz'. It's a brand people love and trust."

"They trust us to not make the stuff in the Philippines!" Shane yells. "I don't like it. This is exactly the kind of thing I didn't want to happen." He thinks for a moment. "Can't we look into other American farms?" he asks. "Sorry, Ben."

"No worries, my friend, we're all in a bind here," Ben says. "Just so ya know, I'm the biggest ramp grower in the northeast. There's some in North Carolina and Tennessee. I don't think they're big enough. None out west, climate's wrong."

"Shit," Shane mutters.

Jacob looks at his young partner. He's learning the downside of being a successful businessman. Sometimes doing the "right" thing isn't easy. Sometimes it's hard to define what "right" even means, exactly. These tough times weren't worth giving it all up, though. It was all worth fighting, and sacrificing for.

"I totally feel what you're feeling, Shane," Jacob says calmly. "But you have to be able to adapt a little. You have a tremendous demand for your product, people love it, and distributors want to sell it all over the place. Poor Ben here can't grow what we need. Some people might be disappointed, but not nearly as many as if they can't get the stuff at all. You might have to make an adjustment." He looks at Shane, who's fidgeting in his seat, trying to come up with a less unsavory solution. Ben is looking out the window, either remembering another time, or trying to figure out where to jam another acre or two of ramp-friendly land.

"You don't want to turn down the Whole Foods deal, do you?" Jacob asks.

"No," Shane says, frustrated. "Dammit. Let's make some calls. Ben, you're okay if we go elsewhere?"

Ben brings himself back into the conversation with a smile. "Shane, you and your spritzy stuff has got everybody and their mother calling ordering ramps. I'm fine. I'm more than fine. Thank you."

"Okay, thanks," Shane says. "Come on, Jacob, let's figure this out."

They get up to leave.

"Good luck, fellas," Ben says.

CHAPTER 9

"Henry!" Sam bellows. "Those new taps?"

The gang has all gathered at Lucky's to watch the MeMeMe interview Shane taped weeks ago, streaming on the big screen tonight. Henry is filling beer glasses, and everyone is happily anticipating the show. There are a few others at some tables in the rear section, but otherwise, they pretty much have the place to themselves.

"Yep, got a whole new kegerator system installed," he says. "The beer tastes like heaven. And all the booths are getting replaced next week."

"Damn," says Gio. "You hit the lottery?"

"I hit the ramp spritz lottery," Henry says, placing beers in front of everyone. "Getting a small piece of that action was the best move I ever made. Don't tell that to my wife. Or my kid."

He smiles and raises a glass, and everyone drinks in honor of the man of the hour.

"To Shane!"

"Thanks, thanks, but I cannot accept the praise," Shane says, as the crowd grumbles disapprovingly. "No, no. Listen. This is because of you, Henry. You were the first one to believe in me, and risk money on me. Money that I didn't have at the time. I'm glad I could pay you back. Thank you. To Henry!"

Everyone raises a glass and toasts again.

"Okay, okay, jeez," Sam butts in. "If you two rich pricks would stop spritzing all over each other for a second so we can fire up the show, that'd be great, okay?"

Everyone laughs, and Jacob clicks the TV on with a remote. The opening to the MeMeMe webcast-gone-broadcast show plays on the bar's main monitor. It's full of Internet-like graphics and visuals, clearly aimed at the progressive, "not one fuck was given" crowd.

"Oh, man, I'm nervous," Shane says.

"You are fine," Zora says. "You're a rock star."

"You said the girl, Bristol, was cool, right?" Sam asks.

"Yeah," says Shane. "She seemed really nice."

"You're good, then," Sam says.

"Okay, here we go…" says Henry.

After the opening sequence, Bristol Hart appears and begins talking to the camera. Her commentary is interspersed with video clips of Shane making his product and working at his office, and also headlines, magazine covers, and articles featuring Shane.

BRISTOL: *Twenty-seven-year-old Brooklynite Shane Foster has done what many other young locals have tried to do, and failed. He's* turned his hand-crafted small-batch artisanal food business into a large, and very profitable, one…

Jacob pats Shane on the back.

…*With a rumored seven-figure deal with Whole Foods, we do mean VERY profitable…*

Sam's eyes widen. Gio's jaw drops. Shane looks down at his Converse sneakers. He looks up only when he hears his own voice coming from the TV.

SHANE: *I've been very fortunate. It goes to show, anyone can be successful if you're honest, and don't try to screw your customers.*

Everyone claps, smiles, and giggles at Shane's grand debut. Zora kisses him on the cheek. He looks around meekly.

BRISTOL: *Shane would have you believe that he's keeping with the proud Brooklyn artisanal traditions of supporting the local community, and putting quality and pride above the bottom line. But is he?*

Zora's smile drops instantly. She looks at Shane, concerned. His mouth opens slightly and freezes. His face loses a shade of color as he sees himself appear on camera again. His friends silently watch, wondering what is about to happen.

SHANE: *Citizen Shane's Ramp Spritz is made locally, from locally grown vegetables, and we package it right here in the city.*

BRISTOL: *Well, that certainly sounds fabulous. But MeMeMe has obtained documents linking a certain man-bun millionaire's company with a ramp farm in... the Philippines?*

A close-up of the contract with the Filipino ramp farm appears on the screen. A sad trombone sound effect, paired with an unfortunately timed still shot of Shane looking idiotic, hammers the point home.

BRISTOL: *Better call New York's Bravest, Shaney, looks like your pants are on fire...*

On the TV screen, special effect flames shoot up from the direction of Shane's pants, paired with the sound of a woman shrieking.

...Our topknot tycoon may need a Google Maps update, because last we checked, the Philippines are NOT local..."

Shane emerges from his shock long enough to say, "We made that deal after the interview. I wasn't lying. What the fuck?"

Zora puts an arm around him and rubs his shoulder sympathetically. Bristol continues.

"...MeMeMe has also learned that the Filipino farm is selling the produce to Mr. Foster at a much lower price than the local farmer he used to buy from..."

"He couldn't... he didn't want... he didn't have space," Shane stammers quietly, to no one in particular. "We had to outsource. We had to."

"*...So, our local hero seems to have made a choice. Profit comes before local pride, even if it means taking jobs overseas. So the next time you crack open a bottle of Citizen Shane's Ramp Spritz, thinking it's a locally grown artisanal product, remember, its main ingredient is grown on a massive farm somewhere in the Philippines.*"

"This fucking..." Jacob says, and cuts himself off.

"*Probably grown and picked by children, working for fifty cents a day, so that hero hipster Shane Foster can buy designer clothes.*"

Shane appears on the screen again.

"*Pra-da!*" he says, flaunting his shirt for the camera.

"You've got to be kidding me," he says to the screen, defeated.

Henry clicks off the TV.

"Why would she..." Shane says. "Why would she do that?"

"I really hate people sometimes," Jacob says.

"I mean, I didn't do anything," Shane says. He thinks for a moment and looks at Zora. "Did I?"

"No. Of course not," she says. "You are producing and providing something people want. And making money as a result." She points angrily at the TV. "*They* are producing and peddling hate."

"I bought one nice shirt," Shane says, still shell-shocked. "For forty dollars. For the interview." He laughs, confused and embarrassed. "I guess that was stupid."

"Dude, stop beating yourself up," Gio says.

"But they are treating me like... they edited what I... they just told everyone I was... like, a rich, greedy asshole. But I'm not. I live in Bushwick. I own *A* tie. What the fuck?"

Everyone is quiet, not sure how to respond to this unexpected change of atmosphere. Henry quickly starts filling shot glasses with Jameson's.

"You know," he says, "I heard about a book, I think it's like two thousand pages long, so I never read it, but I hear shit like this happened in it. Eventually all the ass kickers in the world just got fed up with other people's bullshit, and you know what they all did?"

"What?" asks Gio.

Henry takes a moment and pans the room, looking everyone in the eye dramatically, and says, "SHOTS! Fuck 'em! Cheers all!"

Zora says, "I don't think that's what hap—"

"To SHANE!" Henry bellows, and everyone joins in.

"To Shane," they say in relative unison, raising their glasses.

They drink. Shane looks confused, pale and beaten, but forces a smile.

Shane and Zora arrive at Shane's apartment, which is now their home.

"Hi, Reagan," Shane says as they open the door. He's in a slightly better mood than he'd been at the bar, partially attributable to the generous amounts of whiskey doled out after the MeMeMe broadcast.

"Hi," Zora says. "The monster behave?"

"Oh yeah," Reagan says. "Not a peep."

Shane and Zora are still coming to terms with the fact that, for the next eighteen or so years, they will never return to an empty home. Reagan, their babysitter, is a pleasant enough but tough-looking girl, wearing ripped jeans and a nose ring. She closes her laptop and gets up as they arrive.

"Great," Shane says, fumbling for his wallet. "What'd we say, fifteen?"

"You got it, Mr. Foster," Reagan says.

"Oh, God, it's Shane," Shane answers.

"Okay, yeah," Reagan says. "Fifteen, Shane."

"Here you go," he replies, peeling off some bills. "Three hours, that's forty-five plus twenty for a cab, and an extra five for... beer?"

"I'm eighteen," Reagan says dryly. Zora shakes her head and smiles.

"Oh, right. Well, for pizza then. Here you go," he says, handing her the money. "Thanks."

Reagan takes the money and holds it for a minute. She gives Shane an odd look.

"Thanks," she finally says. "Nice shirt."

Shane looks at his untucked Gap button-down and says, "Uh, thanks?"

"Later," Reagan says, and walks briskly out the apartment door.

"Bye," Zora calls. Once the door slams, she and Shane exchange slightly confused looks.

"That was weird," Shane says. "Nice shirt?"

Zora, realizing what's happening, looks down at her feet.

"Zora? Wha—" Shane says, realizing as well. "Oh shit. She watched." He pauses, bites his lip, and shakes his head in disgust. "Goddammit!"

"Shh!" Zora says. "Don't wake Hope."

"She thinks I short-changed her. She thinks I'm rich. And cheap. And she just watched—" A look of terror comes over Shane's face as he bolts toward their bedroom. Zora runs behind him.

"Shane! What!?"

Shane opens the door, quickly races to the crib, and looks inside. Baby Hope appears to be sleeping peacefully on her back with one arm extended over her head.

"Is she okay?" Shane says, panicking. "Does she look okay?!"

"Shane!" Zora whispers loudly. "Calm down."

Shane reaches in and gently touches Hope's head and chest. Hope wriggles and cries for a moment.

"Shane! She's fine! Stop it!" Zora says, trying not to raise her voice.

Shane breathes deeply and tries to calm himself.

"Okay. Okay," he says, still not quite okay. He takes Zora's hand and they leave the room. Once in the living room, Shane begins pacing.

"Shit," he finally says. "She knows where we live. Does she have a key?"

"No!" Zora says. "Calm down. She doesn't have a key."

"But we left her one in case of an emergency," Shane says. He spots the key on the counter and picks it up, inspecting it. "What if she made a copy?"

"You're being crazy," Zora says. "But we can change the locks if it will make you feel better. I really don't think the babysitter is going to break into our apartment."

"Probably not, but you don't think she's going to tell all her friends about this? She's babysitting for the fucking 'Spritz Prince of New York.' She's eighteen. Who knows what kind of friends she has? Yes, we change the locks. Tomorrow. And after that damn piece tonight, we should get a new deadbolt. There are some weirdos around here, and now everyone's gonna know that their neighbor in 7B is a rich asshole."

"Shane!" Zora yells, not so much to scold him but just to get her life partner back on track. As paranoid as Shane is acting at the moment, she knows there is an important and frightening logic beneath his boozy panic. She's seen how some people can get when they feel others have obtained the success and fortune they themselves deserve. Her father left his entire family for a bottle and a Mexican beach rather than stay and live life as an unsuccessful writer, relegated to the lowly status of "father." She won't be too careful in protecting her own daughter from the spiteful actions of the unreasonably unfulfilled.

Shane seems to snap out of it. "Stop it," Zora says. "You are not an asshole. Everything's fine. You're doing right by your family. We can get a deadbolt. First thing tomorrow. Okay? We should get some rest now."

"Yes," he says. "I'm sorry. That video has me all fucked up. I'm fucking paranoid."

"It's okay," Zora says soothingly. "You're not altogether wrong. Let's get some sleep and we'll talk about it tomorrow. Come on."

Later they lie in bed, Zora asleep, Shane on his back, wide awake in the pool of light the baby monitor is throwing from its nightstand perch. He's wondering how he's gone from happy bartender to tired, wealthy, paranoid businessman-father in less than a year when he hears a clattering noise from somewhere in the apartment. It's not loud enough to wake Zora, but it startles him, and he bolts upright. Zora stirs, but does not awaken. Shane reaches down quietly, grabs the old golf club that lives under his bed, and exits the bedroom. The noise seemed to have come from the kitchen. Shane creeps cautiously through the darkened apartment toward the sound. As he gets closer, he hears a different noise: a strange, low humming from the far end of the pitch-dark kitchen. It gets louder as he gets closer. He stops at the open doorway, his eyes wide and his jaw taut, gripping the club firmly in one hand. He reaches into the kitchen with the other, and turns on the light.

A plastic, robotic monkey toy has apparently rolled off the table and activated itself into a continuous circular loop of spastic simian break-dancing action, emitting the rhythmic humming noise as it spins spasmodically on the kitchen floor. Shane exhales, walks across the kitchen, picks it up, and turns it off. He rubs his eyes, takes a deep breath, and leans on the table.

"Jesus Christ," he says.

CHAPTER 10

"That's where the ramps get chopped up," Shane says, pointing out some menacing-looking machinery to Sam and Gio. "Sorry it's taken me so long to get you guys out here. Things have been crazy."

"All good," Gio says. "Somebody has to feed the masses."

"Pulverized ramps for all!" Sam adds, laughing.

Shane smiles, then stops along the tour of his massive new processing facility in Brooklyn to wave to a man working the equipment.

"What's up, Martin?" he says.

"Muy bueno, jefe, muy bueno," Martin calls back happily.

"Martin knows how all this stuff works," Shane says to Sam and Gio as he points to a group of large, stainless steel containers, connected by an array of copper tubing and pipes. "That's where the spices get added in."

"What are in those vats?" Gio asks, pointing to a wall of massive metal containers about twenty yards across the room.

"Olive oil," Shane says. "Shit-tons of olive oil."

"Damn, Shane-Dog," Sam says, taking it all in. "Long way from your kitchen in Bushwick." He gestures across the vast plant to a large area, where another set of machinery is being utilized. "What's going on over there?"

"That's Jacob's stuff," Shane says. "Moosetard and Yakabob sauce. The actual yak is processed in Jersey." He gestures to an empty, apparently unused area. "And all that space is for future expansion."

"Damn," Gio says, wide-eyed. "I can't believe all this is yours, man."

"Well, it's not actually mine," Shane replies. "It's some real estate holding firm's in Singapore. I send them checks. After we got the Olive Garden and Macaroni Grill deals, we had to expand quickly."

"Yeah, but, I mean, this business," Gio says. "It's making money. Real money, man. You did it."

Shane pauses and looks around, then says with a flat affect, "Yeah."

"What's wrong, bro?" Sam asks.

"Nothing," Shane says with a sigh. "It's just, I feel like people think I'm different now. Friends, family, neighbors, everyone. That damn MeMeMe website comes up with something new every week. Every success I have, they come up with some new way to shit on me. They can spin anything to make me look like an asshole. And they do. I didn't know people did that, or had the desire to do that to people. It's fucked. I still don't know what they have against me. And the thing is, people love it. I can see it in their eyes when they see me out and around. 'Hey, there's that rich asshole.'"

"As long as they buy your salad stuff," Sam says. "Fuck 'em."

Shane gives him a dismissive look.

"I think you're just being paranoid," Gio says.

"They love the product and hate the guy who makes it," Shane says. "It's fucked, man. I'm the same dude I was behind the bar. Only now I make a great product that people spend their money on."

"Well, if it helps at all," Sam says, "I say you're the same limp-dick you always were. Just with more money."

"Thanks, I guess," Shane says, shoving Sam's shoulder. "But still, I'm not going to let some Internet rag make me look like a capitalist douche. I have a plan."

"What are you thinking?" Sam asks.

"Well," Shane says, "I'm going to do a bunch of stuff that greedy capitalist douches don't do. I'm going to give a big check to charity. And I'm telling the press. Bristol Hart wants to play dirty, I'll play nice. *And* dirty."

"Nice," Gio says, smiling proudly.

"And," Shane adds, "I'm staying in Bushwick."

"Uh, okay," Sam says hesitantly.

"And I'm just not going to, you know, spend a bunch of my money. Not going to go around flaunting it, you know?"

"Well, uh, so…" Sam says. "What are you going to do with it?"

"Don't know," Shane says. "Just hold it in the bank, I guess. Save for Hope's college."

Sam looks around the humming plant and raises an eyebrow. "How many colleges you planning on sending her to?"

"Ha, ha. Whatever," Shane says. "I just don't want to spend it on… stuff."

"That's just weird," Sam says.

"No, it's not," Shane says, getting angry. "Like I said, I never wanted to be rich. And I meant it. This business just sort of happened to me. I have a lot of people working for me now, relying on me, so I'm going to keep it going. But I'm not going to go out and buy mansions and cars and boats. Nothing. I'll show everyone that you can be a successful businessman and not be a douchebag."

"Why don't you want to be rich?" Sam asks.

"Because rich people are assholes," Shane says.

"But you're rich," Sam replies, "whether you buy boats or put the money in the bank. So, either you've proven yourself wrong, or you are, in fact, an asshole."

"Fuck off, Sam," Shane says.

Sam shrugs silently.

"I like it," Gio jumps in. "Be a role model for successful non-douches everywhere."

"Exactly," Shane says.

Gio looks at his watch. "Alright, gents. This has been awesome, but I gotta split. We're recording tonight. What are you up to?"

"Nothing really," Shane says. "I don't think I have any spritz emergencies to deal with today. Yet."

"Want to get a beer?" Sam asks.

"Sure," Shane says.

"Thanks for grabbing a beer with me, man," Sam says, as they settle in at a cocktail table at a Brooklyn bar. "I know you're busy."

"Dude, never too busy to have a pint with you," Shane says, stifling a yawn. "A little tired is all. Hope's teething, which means Daddy ain't sleeping."

"Ha. Gotcha," Sam says, with new focus. "All right, I don't want to waste your time so I'll get to the point. You know I have some apps I'm working on outside the office, right?"

"Yeah, sure. I know."

"Well," he says, smiling. "I think I have a good one."

"Cool," says Shane, perking up. "What is it?"

"It's called Toss."

"Toss?"

"Yeah, Toss. It allows you to take pictures with your iPhone, and literally toss them to another person's phone, like this."

Sam pulls out his phone, snaps a pic of Shane, and flicks the phone towards Shane's, which is sitting on the table. Shane's phone chirps and glows, and the picture appears almost instantaneously on his screen.

"Get the... that is nuts!" Shane says.

"I tested it on some tweens and teens," Sam says. "They go bananas. They all want it."

"I would think so," Shane says. "*I* want it."

"You can set up who you can Toss to and catch Tosses from. It works with GPS coordinates. So long as you know which direction your friend is in, you can toss and catch. Totally customizable, too."

"Awesome," Shane says, smiling proudly. "This is big, man. So what's next?"

"Well. That's kinda why I asked you to get a beer," Sam says, putting his phone down and taking a gulp of liquid courage. "I've got the code all written. The app's ready. It works. I just don't have the... power to get it into the format

Apple needs it to be in for me to officially submit it, and then get it to Apple, pay the lawyers so it doesn't get stolen…"

"You need money," Shane interrupts.

"For this to happen, yes. If I wait to save it, or raise it, technology will change and this app will be obsolete. These things have a small window—"

"How much?" Shane asks calmly.

"I was thinking five. I've got about two in savings that I'll use up. Seven would cover, well, most of it. And I'll pay you back as soon as I possibly can. And every penny would go to the—"

"How about fifty?"

Sam looks up in shock. "You're aware I am talking thousands, right?" he says.

"Yes," Shane says, channeling Jacob. "Fifty grand, don't pay me back, I'll take 5% if you sell the thing."

"Fifty thousand?" Sam asks, wide-eyed.

"Would that help? I don't want any excuses if you don't sell this thing. It's awesome. It needs to be out there."

"Shit, yes," Sam says, excitedly. "I can develop it over multiple platforms, make it auto update, plug and play, yes! I can make it so that Apple won't be able to resist!"

"I'll have the lawyers write something up," Shane says. They shake hands.

"Man," Sam says. "I don't know what to say."

"You should say, 'Who's there?'" Shane says.

"Why?"

Shane's phone buzzes on the table.

"Hold on, it's Zo," he says, answering the phone. "Hey Zo, everything all— What?!" Shane stiffens, and Sam looks at him with concern. "I'm coming," Shane says into the phone. "No, no. Stay inside. I'll be right there." He hangs up and gets up to leave.

"What happened?" Sam asks.

"I gotta go," he says, making his way to the exit. "We'll talk."

"You ran out of sugar, my ass!" Zora yells. "You never even said hello before Shane's business took off! Now you knock on our door five times a week asking for some bullshit! Stop it!"

Standing in the hallway outside Shane's unit, Zora is holding a crying Hope, her full attention on a scraggly-looking, glassy-eyed couple who are also standing in the hall. It's hard to tell if they are in their 30s or 50s. A police officer is positioned between the couple and Zora, attempting to calm them all down, to no avail. The couple lean on the opposite unit's door, smiling menacingly at Zora's distress. A second officer stands a few steps away, in "just in case" position.

"Ma'am, just calm down," says the first officer. "Let's just stay calm and we'll get this all sorted out, okay?"

"Whoa," Shane yells, entering the hallway from the stairwell. "What's going on?!"

"This your husband, ma'am?" the officer asks Zora.

"No. Well, yes," Zora says. It wasn't a time for marital formalities.

"What happened?" Shane asks.

The neighbor lady smiles drearily, revealing several spaces where teeth would traditionally be, and says, "We just come by to borruh some sugar. Your wahf here goes all ape-shit on us."

"Oh, come on! I gave you sugar yesterday. How much do you need?!" Zora shouts. "What are you up to? You casing the place? We don't have diamonds and gold lying around – go to Tribeca! And leave us alone!"

"Okay, calm down, Ms. Zora," the officer says. "We're gonna figure this out."

"When!? Right after one of these creeps breaks in and beats the shit out of one of us?!"

"Okay, take it easy, Zo," Shane says firmly, patting Hope gently on the head and gesturing into the apartment. "Get inside with her. I'll handle this."

"Thas right," the neighbor husband chimes in, so calm in such a tense situation that it's eerie. "Control your bit… woman."

"What did you say?" Shane says, shifting gears.

"Okay, don't," the police officer warns, as his partner takes a step forward. "Zora, please go inside," he says, loudly now. He addresses the neighbors. "And Mr. and Mrs…?"

"Smith," says the man.

"Bullshit," says Zora.

"Inside. Please," Shane says. Zora goes into the apartment and consoles Hope, but leaves the door open.

"Mr. and Mrs. Smith," the officer says to the neighbors. "Why don't you get home and I'll come and get a statement from you later."

"Sure thing, Mr. Officer," the man says. "Night Zora, Shane. Ya'll be good citizens now, ya hear?"

With this, the man turns the knob on the door directly across the hall. He and the lady enter the unit, and close the door behind them.

"They live right there?" the officer asks after a moment.

"Yes," Shane says, weighing his staunch Bushwick pride and toughness with his current fear and embarrassment. "It's a transitional neighborhood."

"Mmm-hmm," the officer says, pulling out a notepad.

"Can you do anything?" Shane asks.

"I can't arrest them for asking for sugar."

"But you know that's bullshit," Zora says from inside the apartment, holding a much calmer Hope. "They're up to something. As soon as Shane's business deal hit the news, those two snakes started slithering around. They are always high on God knows what, and their druggie friends are always coming around too. I'm scared as shit."

"I will go talk to them and tell them to get their sugar elsewhere," the officer says. "And I will file a report. Call if they bother you again."

"They live RIGHT THERE!" Zora yells, pointing, defeated, on the verge of tears. "If they want to do anything, they'll have time to do it five times before you guys arrive. We've gotta get out of here, Shane. I can't take it."

"Okay," he says, quietly thinking of options. "I'll think of something."

"Okay, folks," the officer says. "Get some rest. I will stay in the neighborhood for a while. That's all I can do for now. You'll be fine. Try to relax. Have a good night."

As the officers knock and enter the apartment across the hall, Shane and Zora head into their unit and close the door. Zora puts Hope in her crib and settles her down. They close the bedroom door and head to the kitchen.

"I'm sorry, Shane, but I can't take it," Zora finally says, still upset. With Hope safe in her crib, Zora's protective instincts subside and she suddenly finds herself needing a little protection herself. She hugs Shane, crying softly.

"Sorry," she says.

"For what?" he asks, wiping a tear from her cheek. "Stop it. Those two are fucked up. I'm so sorry that happened. You don't deserve that."

"*We* don't deserve that. You know when you *know* something is up?" she says. "Well, something is up with those two."

"I know. I believe you. I'm just not sure what to do about it."

"Shane!" she says emphatically. "We have to leave! I mean, I love living in Bushwick, but I'm starting to think I love the idea of loving Bushwick more than I actually love Bushwick. I'm sure it's going to be a totally safe neighborhood someday, but it's not today. And we have Hope. And money, which apparently puts a target on us. We have to get out of here."

"White flight," Shane says firmly, shaking his head. "No. We aren't leaving."

"It's not white flight!" Zora says, trying to keep her voice down. "Those crackheads across the hall are white! Leaving Bushwick might look racist, but it's not, and frankly, I don't care what it *looks* like. It's right to want to protect your child from danger, no matter what color it is. Now we get out of here or, I don't know, I can't be here with Hope, with those two lurking around. And remember the babysitter we were worried about, Reagan?"

"Yeah," Shane says. "What about her?"

"I called her once, and she said she doesn't come to this neighborhood anymore and hung up. It was weird. Ugh. Shane, I'm scared."

"Okay, okay. Where would you like to go?" Shane asks, more trying to ensnare her in some logical trap he's created in his mind than get an actual suggestion.

"There are safe, nice towns everywhere," she says. "I don't care. As long as we're safe."

"You mean a rich town," he says accusingly.

"Shane!" Zora says, almost yelling now. "I don't give a flying fuck if it's rich, poor, black, white, Republican, Democrat, Islamic, monarchy, or commune! I only care about the safety of us and our daughter. Not how we appear to other people who aren't fully paying attention. The police *appear* to be able to protect us, but we know that's not true. We might appear to be racists, but we know that's not true. So drop the utopian hipster dream, and start figuring out a safe place for your family to live."

Shane goes over options in his mind. He gets an idea. "Maybe I'll get a, you know, a—"

"Gun?!" Zora says, almost laughing. "You're afraid of looking like a white flight-er, but think it's acceptable to shoot and kill what you aren't fleeing from?! Shane. Come on."

Shane quickly realizes it was an idea he had not fully thought through.

"Ugh. I know. I just… I fucking hate Westchester," he says.

Zora smiles and says calmly, "I think you hate the *idea* of Westchester, just like you love the *idea* of Bushwick. It's not about what we like or hate, or think is cool, or lame, or in good conscience, or socially acceptable. It may have been our job once to figure that out, but we have a daughter now, Shane. Her well-being is our job, and two desperate creeps live ten feet from her."

"I hear you," Shane says. "I just think there is something to be said for, I don't know, exposing her to all kinds of people, you know."

"There's a difference between exposing her to all kinds of people and voluntarily living across the hall from danger. I'm not some kind of elitist or racist, Shane. Or, you know what? If doing what I think is best to keep my daughter safe means I am, then maybe I am. I don't care. I need her to not be here anymore."

Shane looks at her. He hears what she's saying, but something compels him to resist.

"Okay. I hear you," he says. "You're right. I just… I'm just not sure I'm ready yet, okay?"

"No! That is *not* okay!"

Shane sees a look in Zora's eyes he has never seen before. It's not sadness, not desperation, not hate. It's determination. And anger.

"If what just happened does not make you ready, then you never will be," she says, through clenched teeth. "And I'm not going to keep my daughter in danger because her father really hates Westchester! And—"

She cuts herself off.

"What?" Shane asks angrily. "And what?"

"No. Nothing."

"Zora, you just threatened to take my daughter from me. It can't be worse than that. And what?"

"You can afford it, Shane!" she says angrily, quickly, like a verbal rubber band snapping as it's stretched to its highest tension point, then let go. As strange as it was, this was the first time Zora had ever mentioned the money. The elephant had remained invisible since it entered the room six months ago, and they were both afraid to bring it up, for fear of it breaking something precious if exposed. Well, here it was now, in the open, exposed by a mother's desire to protect her child.

"You can afford it, Shane," Zora says, calmer now. "You have the means to keep your daughter safe. You are one of the lucky ones. Not like those two across the hall. Maybe someday they will get their shit together and help themselves and those they care about, but it's not our job to wait for others to figure it out. You already have. You created something great, so you have the resources to keep your family safe. You did that. And if you have the means to keep us safe, and choose not to, well, I don't know."

Zora, although calmer now, is speaking with a resolve that simultaneously frightens Shane and makes him love her even more. He can't quite bring himself to look her in the eye, as he's working toward a difficult epiphany.

"Okay, okay. I know. You're right," he says, understanding, accepting, but dejected still.

Zora hugs him. "We got this," she says.

"Why the fuck is this happening?" Shane asks. "I never wanted any of this."

Zora's face turns hard as she takes him by the hand and vigorously walks him into the bedroom, where Hope is asleep in her crib.

"You didn't want this either!" she says in an emphatic whisper, pointing at Hope. "So let's stop whining about what we did or didn't want, and make the most of what we have, and for fuck's sake, not screw it up!"

Shane takes a long look at Hope, and as he does, Zora speaks to him very softly.

"Shane, I love you. And I've seen you create two beautiful things in the short time I've known you. She is one of them. I don't think you knew you had it in you, but you did. Let me introduce you to yourself. You are not Shane Foster who comes home to crying daughters and screaming mothers and police in his hallway. You are Shane Foster who comes home to his family, safe and sound, just as you left them. Because you earned that."

Shane looks up at Zora. Somehow being harassed by crackheads has made Shane love her even more than he thought possible.

"I understand," he says. "I love you. Thanks. I just, I just don't know if I love… the new me."

Zora takes his hands firmly and looks him in the eye. "There is nothing wrong, immoral, or ignoble about protecting your family. And you can. That's not a bad thing, Citizen Shane. Not at all. Smile."

Shane looks at Zora, then down at Hope, who wiggles and gurgles in her sleep. He smiles and nods slowly, and hugs Zora for a long time.

CHAPTER 11

"So I guess all we were wondering was, if, hypothetically we did want to leave Brooklyn and buy a house, well, is that a good idea?"

Shane is fidgeting on the slick, black leather couch in his accountant's office in Midtown. Zora looks at him and smiles— partially from the excitement of this "grown-up" move they're making, and partially in amused sympathy watching Shane struggle with the notion. She pats him on the knee and nods her head reassuringly.

"I mean, we don't need anything too big," Shane continues. "We just have one kid. And she's tiny."

Sal Romano has been guiding couples and individuals through the mad world of personal finance for twenty years. A smile crosses his tanned face, and wrinkles the skin around his small mouth and above his black Oliver Peoples frames.

"Well," Sal says, leafing through a file of papers, "I've gone over the numbers. You have a large amount of cash on hand for the down payment, and you have a solid monthly income. It only seems to be increasing as time goes on, so the future looks quite secure."

"Phew," Shane says. "I mean, I kinda knew. But it's good to hear. So we can buy a house?"

"Yes," Sal smiles again. "I think you can comfortably look for something in the six to seven range."

Zora perks up. Shane exhales. "Good, okay. Seven hundred grand," he says. "That's about what I figured. The property taxes in Westchester are crazy, but I think we can find a nice small three-bedroom, maybe a cond-"

"Six to seven million, Mr. Foster," Sal interrupts.

All four of Zora and Shane's eyes widen.

"Excuse me?" Shane says.

"I'm looking at your ledgers," Sal says, and then holds them out for Shane to look at. "These are yours, right?"

"Yes," Shane says, looking them over. As he registers the dollar figures they contain, he adds, "Jesus."

"Didn't know how well you were doing?" Sal asks, still smiling the smile of a proud father rather than that of an accountant who just landed a whale.

"I mean, I did, but my partner Jacob sorta does the money stuff," Shane says, as Sal nods knowingly. "I figured if I had the rent every month and could buy beer and baby formula, I was doing good. I never really looked at the numbers."

"That's okay," Sal says reassuringly. "Jacob pays me to do that."

Shane laughs. "I'll remember to thank him. Again," he says, shaking his head, still swimming in disbelief.

"So," Zora says. "We can afford a seven-million-dollar house?"

"Yes," Sal answers. "Comfortably."

"My God," Shane says, uncomfortably.

"Well," Sal says, "It's smart to diversify your assets, in case the business ever does take a turn… stocks, bonds, etc. We can talk more about that in the future. But real estate is a safe, solid investment, especially in a desirable area like Westchester.

"But seven million?" Shane says. "We don't need that much house."

"You're welcome to buy one for less," Sal says, "but then the government is just going to bang you for almost fifty percent of what you don't spend on it. Every year."

"Really?" Shane asks.

"Yep. Capital gains tax."

"We get, like, penalized for making money? Having a successful business?" Zora asks.

"Well, not exactly," Sal says, "The government is okay with you making money, as long as spend it right away."

Zora's face contorts in confusion. "But then there's sales tax on everything we spend it on."

"Oh yes, that's true," Sal says, contemplatively. "I guess they get you either way. Might as well buy a mansion."

"Ugh," Shane says. "The press is going to crucify me."

"They already do," Zora points out. "And you live in a $1,200 a month one-bedroom apartment with a leaky toilet."

"And if I may," Sal says, "remember your alternative. Your company shows a seven million dollar profit at the end of the year. It's all public information."

"Shit," Shane says.

"A profit of which you would only actually get to keep half," Sal says.

Shane looks dejectedly at Sal, who throws his hands up and shrugs. "I know a PR guy I can put you in touch with. I just do money."

"Hey," Shane says, having a realization. "What if we look for something a little cheaper, and make a big charity contribution as well? That's deductible, right? Set off some of the ill will. I think that's a good thing to do, right?"

Zora nods in agreement.

"Sure," Sal says. "You can write that all off, and it's certainly commendable to give back to the community. I can help you do that."

"Okay. Great," Shane says to Sal. He thinks for a moment and turns to Zora. "Let's go house shopping."

"And now, I'd like to introduce our guest of honor, Shane Foster!"

Ruth Harper, a sharply dressed African-American woman, stands at a podium, speaking to a large group of people gathered in a park outside the entrance area of a public works type building. Shane and Zora are passing a grumpy Hope back and forth in the honored guest section of the seated audience. Reporters and photographers stand along the side of the crowd, snapping pictures and taking notes.

"Shane had only one request for me regarding his introduction," Ruth says, "and that was to not call him Mr. Foster."

Laughs and giggles ripple through the crowd.

"But seriously," she continued, "Shane's generous donation has brought tremendous and necessary improvements to the Bushwick Angels Community Center for underprivileged youth. Thank you so much, Mr… Shane."

Shane gently passes Hope to Zora, grabs an oversized posterboard "check" leaning against his chair, rises, and brings it to the podium. The large print on the check reads "one million dollars." The crowd stands, applauding. The press snaps pictures. Bristol Hart smiles slyly as she writes in her notepad. Shane sees her as he settles at the podium, and raises an eyebrow.

"Hi, everyone. I'm really glad to join all of you today to celebrate the revitalization of this fabulous and vital youth center. Zora and I have lived here for years, and we've come to love the community we call home. As you know, I've obviously been tremendously fortunate lately, and when you suddenly find yourself with a lot of money, you find yourself with a lot of decisions to make about what to do with it. I'm no financial guru, so please, do not take any advice from me, but I can tell you one thing. There are a lot of things you can do with your money, and a lot of people telling you what you should and should not do with it. But in the end, you have to do what you feel is right. That goes for money, or anything really. That's what I did. I'm not buying boats, or joining golf clubs or investing in hedge funds. I'm giving it to a good cause. This cause. This community."

The crowd erupts into applause. Charm and money are a formidable combination. Bristol scribbles in her notepad as Zora smiles uncomfortably.

"And everyone I meet these days wants to know one thing," Shane continues. "They want the answer. The answer to the big question. They come up to me and they ask, 'Shane. Mr. Foster. You have all this success, all this money, this big business, your big processing plant, your beautiful girlfriend, your beautiful daughter, and I gotta ask you, I gotta ask you one thing. What on earth is a ramp?'"

The crowd cracks up as Zora smiles. Bristol, furiously scribbling, shakes her head without looking up from her notepad.

CHAPTER 12

Real estate agent Mary Middleton extracts the correct key from a small collection stashed in her possibly genuine Prada bag and inserts it into the front door lock. She has real estate agent blonde hair, and wears a real estate knee-length skirt and a real estate shiny white top. She opens the heavy door and gestures Shane and Zora into the empty and enormous foyer. Hope is strapped to Zora in a baby carrier contraption, her head bobbing around as she takes in the vast expanse with wide baby-eyes. Even though Mary has done this hundreds of times, twice today, she displays the enthusiasm of someone who has never seen a house before, no less sold one, as they begin the tour.

"Ooh, now this is a bit of a more classic layout with the closed floor plan," she says as she glides from room to room. "You have your living room here, and the dining room there… and then, my favorite… here."

"My goodness," Zora says, as they enter the kitchen, which is larger than their current home. The stainless steel appliances gleam like skate blades, and a granite-topped chef's island stands majestically in the center of it all.

"Wow," Shane adds, taking it all in. "I wish we cooked."

"This one has the six bedrooms upstairs," Mary says. "And a bar and movie theater in the basement."

"Movie theater?" Shane asks.

"Well, it's a small one," Mary says, almost apologetically. "Seats maybe twenty or so."

Hope makes an incomprehensible baby sound, which Zora acknowledges with wide eyes. "Ah, yes. Peppa Pig party! Yes, Hopeyboo!"

Shane smiles at them and rolls his eyes affectionately. "How much is this one?" he asks.

"They're asking six. I'm sure we can get them down closer to five and a half."

"My God, that's a lot of money." He looks at the convection oven and built-in wine refrigerator, then pleadingly at Zora. "Zo- really?"

"Shane, we've been through this," she says, looking up from Hope and getting serious. "You have the money. You can either have a badass movie theater in your basement and a new bedroom to sleep in every night of the week, or live across the hall from Breaking Bad and give a few million bucks to the government every year to buy bombs with. Whichever makes you happier, babe."

Zora had apparently run out of patience, and fucks, regarding the subject.

Embarrassed, Shane looks at Mary, who has suddenly become very interested in an invisible stain on the granite counter.

He looks around the room, and out to the rooms beyond, and can't believe what he's seeing. He doesn't feel right even standing in this massive, luxurious home, much less buying it. He also feels like he's being forced into a situation outside that which he would choose. He hates people who buy houses like this. The right thing to do, apparently, was what he always thought was wrong. He starts getting that weird dreamlike sensation again, not exactly a nightmare, but not quite real either. He wants to snap out of it. He doesn't want to be there. But what other options does he have? Life, his life, was going to forge ahead regardless of how he thought it was supposed to play out. He could either fight it, or try to figure out how to embrace it. He takes a deep breath and exhales.

"Right. Fine," he says to Zora. "Do you like it?"

"I love it." Zora's face lights up with what Mary instantly recognizes as the "this is the one" smile.

"When is it available?" Shane asks Mary.

"It's ready to go. The family moved back to London. I think they just want to unload it as fast as possible. And with the funds you have available, they will be quite motivated."

"Right, okay," Shane says, still unable to commit.

"Shane?" Zora asks. "Do you want to see the theater?"

"No," he says.

"Please don't be sad."

Mary jumps in. "You can put in an offer and see what they come back with. Nothing's legally binding yet."

Shane thinks for another moment, smiles, and nods.

"Okay," Mary says.

Zora runs to Shane and hugs him, as best as she can with a baby strapped to her.

"Careful," he says, as he holds her. "Don't crush Hope."

"You gotta be fucking kidding me," Jacob says, looking at his computer monitor. Shane is at his own desk across their vast shared office, at the processing plant in Brooklyn.

"What?" Shane asks.

"Our friend is at it again."

"Who?"

Jacob sends Shane a G-Chat with a link to an article in it. Shane clicks on it, warily.

"Oh no," he says, as the familiar colors and layout of the "MeMeMe" site pop up on his monitor. The main headline reads: *"Manbun Mansion: Brooklyn's Spritz Prince Buys Palace and Writes Checks to Charities While His Aunt Can't Pay for Diabetes Treatment."*

"Mother fu— what aunt?!" Shane yells.

Jacob quickly scans the article.

"Lorraine?" he says. "In Tampa?"

"What the… really?" Shane says. "I think I met her *once*— when I was six! I didn't know she had diabetes! I didn't know she was still alive! How did they even find her?"

"Sorry, man," Jacob says. "This chick has it out for you."

"I don't get it," Shane says, defeated. "I didn't do anything to her."

"I don't think it's about that. It's not personal. It's a game to her. Numbers, money, clicks. She thrives on them like an addiction."

"Well, she obviously has an audience that eats it up," Shane says angrily. "I just don't understand why. All I did was make some stuff that *they* all wanted and encouraged me to make and sell. Now that I did, everything I do is evil. What the fuck?"

As he scrolls down the webpage, he sees a paparazzi-type shot of himself and Zora kissing on their front lawn, as movers move boxes into their new home.

"Jesus, they got a picture of us at the house. They forced us up there! They kept telling our neighbors in Bushwick how rich and greedy I am! I didn't even want to move!"

"You committed what is now considered the biggest sin in America," Jacob says.

"Terrorism?" Shane says, confused.

"Getting rich."

Shane picks up his desk phone and dials. Jacob walks over and sits on the corner of Shane's desk.

"Trish, can you please call MeMeMe and find out who exactly Aunt Lorraine in Tampa is? And if I am in fact actually related to her, please send her a check for her goddamn diabetes treatment. Thanks."

"Shouldn't do that, man," Jacob says.

"What, and then read later how my greed *killed* my poor diabetic Aunt Lorraine? No thanks."

"Listen," Jacob says. "They have all the ammunition they need to get to you. Your money, and your guilt for having it. They can keep getting to you until you give one of them up."

Shane stares across the room. He's angry.

"May I suggest it not be the money," Jacob says.

Shane thinks for a bit. "I thought life was supposed be easier with a shit-ton of money," he says softly, to Jake, and the universe. "I mean, I always hated rich people, but I at least thought I understood why they did what they did. To have an easy life. I thought they were lazy. Just being rich instead of working hard in life, you know? Lemme tell you, it's not easy. I got a kid and her mom at home, and I'm here at work worrying about reporters and photographers and accountants and sick aunts in Florida that I didn't know I had. I'm supposed to be making goddamn salad dressing."

Shane's computer dings, signaling a new G-Chat. It's from Gio.

Hey man, what's up? I wrote some new jingles. I emailed you the MP3s. Want to check them out? See if you can use one for the business. Of course they need polish, but that costs beaucoup bucks. Know anyone who has some? ;)

"And friends who all need money," Shane says. "I gotta get out of here."

"All right, man. Just take it easy," Jacob says. "Go hug your baby girl. She loves you and knows you're a good guy. And she's not asking for money."

"Not yet, anyway," Shane says, as he gets up and leaves.

Shane is feeling tense and dismayed as he drives home in his new Honda CR-V. He plays the jingles Gio sent out of the Bluetooth speaker system. They're awful. Shane grimaces, switches on the radio, and turns the volume up. His phone rings. "Gio" appears on the car's display screen.

"Fuck!"

Shane takes a deep breath and hits a button on the steering wheel, answering the call on the integrated speaker system.

"G-Money, what's up?" he says, trying to sound the opposite of how he's feeling.

"Hey, man," Gio says. "Just checking if you got those jingles, man. I've been working on them for a while and I was psyched to hear what you thought."

Shane is angry. He's squeezing the steering wheel and biting his tongue. He swerves to avoid a cyclist, who yells and gives him the finger.

"Yeah, I listened," he says.

"Okay," Gio says. Shane doesn't respond. "Aaand?"

"What? You want to know what I think?"

"Um, yeah. You okay, man?"

"Yeah, it's just that I'm not a marketing guy, or an ad guy, or a music guy, so I'm not sure why you would send these to me, to get my opinion on them."

"Okay…"

"I'm not sure you want to know what I think so much as pay you for your jingles."

"What the fuck, dude? What's got your dick in a knot?"

"Gio, I love you man, but be honest. Do you really want my opinion? Is that really what you want?"

"Yes, man. That's really what I want. That's why I gave them to you. What the fuck, Shane?"

"Okay. They suck, okay!" Shane yells at the top of his lungs. "They're horrible! And since I know why you really sent them to me, no, I'm not going to buy them! No one is! That's my opinion! And I'll throw in some friendly career advice. I'm not sure music is the field you should be in. I'm not sure you have the talent to compete and make a living, and you would probably do better in a different field. There. That's my opinion."

He drives in silence, breathing heavily, heart pounding. He's about to speak when Gio says calmly, "Damn, dude. I just, fine, I know that you gave Sam some money, so I thought we were friends, man, that's all."

Shane winces. He wishes Gio hadn't found out about the loan, but then again, how wouldn't he? Secrets between friends become fifty-thousand-dollar ones when one friend is a millionaire.

"Friendship doesn't make a bad investment a good idea, Gio," Shane says, still trying unsuccessfully to relax his breathing. "Or a bad jingle a good one. Sam's app was good... no, it was great! These jingles are not. They're bad. It's not just about friendship, man. I can't give my money to everyone I know that has some crappy product they want to sell."

"Dude, I don't know why you're being like this, man. I know my shit is good. *Everyone* tells me it is."

"How many of these people who say how great your stuff is actually buy it?"

"None yet," Gio says quietly, after a long pause.

"One thing I've learned in this business I've gotten myself into," Shane says, "there is one sure way to know, without a doubt, if your stuff is any good, and that's if people are willing to pay for it. You may think your work is God's gift to Earth, but if no one wants any part of it, well, join the dreamer's club. So you can be mad at me if you want, but realize that what's going on is that no one actually wants your jingles. If they did, they would buy them. Everything else is a smoke show. I'm just the only one being honest with you."

"Fine!" Gio says loudly, angrily. "Since we're being *honest*, you've changed, man! You've changed since you got all this money. You think you're all hot shit now, judging me, telling me I have no talent. Like you do? Fuck you, man. You make fucking salad dressing! Fuck you and your big old damn house in the 'burbs and fuck your shiny new Mercedes SUV too. Call me if you think I've found enough talent to be your friend!"

He hangs up.

"It's a Honda," Shane says to no one. "You didn't want my friendship. You wanted my money. *You* changed."

The phone rings again. Shane answers.

"Hey, Zo."

"Hey," Zora says. "You okay? The office said you left."

"Yeah, fine. Rough day is all."

"The business okay?"

"Business is fine. Better than ever. It's just, shit, I don't know. Life."

"Sorry," Zora says, sympathetically. "Well, sounds like you might not be in a socializing mood, but a couple dropped by from up the street to say hi. They're really nice. Can you grab a bottle of wine?"

"Oh no, Zora, really?" Shane says pleadingly. "I can't tonight."

"Shane, they are here. Would you like me to ask your new neighbors to leave because you're grumpy?"

Shane takes a deep breath.

"White or red?" he asks through gritted teeth.

Zora is sitting in the sparsely furnished living room of their new home with Everett and Ashley Casey, a 30-something, refined-looking couple. When Shane enters the living room he nearly drops the bottles of wine he has brought home upon seeing them. He knows them. He can't remember how. But it's not a positive past interaction vibe he's getting.

"Whoa, you okay?" Everett says, getting up to help Shane with the bottles.

"Yes," Shane says, still a little shaken. He places the bottles down in the kitchen. "Sorry. I'm Shane."

"Everett," he says, as they shake hands. He's tall and wiry with thick blond '90s hair that permanently falls over one eye. He gestures to his wife. "This is Ashley."

She gets up, shakes Shane's hand and flips her sandy blonde ponytail over a shoulder of her white oxford button down.

"Nice meeting you," she says. "Thanks so much for bringing wine. Not that Zora hasn't been sufficiently entertaining us."

"Ha. Yes, she does. Is," Shane says awkwardly. He remembers Ashley's voice. Damn, why can't he place these two?

"Hon. You okay?" Zora asks Shane.

"Yes. Sorry. Just a rough day." He's scanning Ashley and Everett's faces, trying to remember, but also trying not to look weird doing so.

"Zora tells us you guys met in a bar. How refreshing!" she says genuinely. "You were a bartender?"

"Yeah. Till about a year ago."

"Where?" she asks.

"Lucky's. Prospect Heights. You probably never—"

"Oh. My. God," she interrupts, putting her head down.

"Ash?" Everett asks. "What is it?"

Zora looks at Shane, and sort of shrugs. Shane feels the blood rush from his face, as he's apparently about to have his memory of their past acquaintance jogged.

"This is so embarrassing," Ashley says hesitantly. "You were the bartender there the night Everett and I came in shitfaced after that charity fundraiser last fall."

A wave of memory passes from Ashley to Everett, and finally to Shane. They both turn a shade lighter.

"Oh, no," Everett says, looking at Shane. "You're right. I think." Everett squints, trying to remember. Shane hopes he doesn't. "I don't remember much of the evening, unfortunately."

"That's right," Shane says, stepping cautiously into this social minefield. "I'm sorry I did—"

"We are *so* sorry about that," Ashley says, wincing. "We were drunken boobs, as I recall. I hope you threw us out before we did anything really stupid."

Shane, expecting to be offering the apology instead of receiving it, says, "Oh no. You guys were fine. No big deal at all. I think, I just… we were closed, was all."

"Oh, okay. Phew, that's a relief!" Everett says. "That was the last time we swigged straight tequila from a flask! We finally got away from the kids for a night, and the event was so boring…"

"And dry," Ashley adds, rolling her eyes.

"We were desperate!" Everett yells dramatically.

The four neighbors laugh at the memory, relieved it didn't cause any lasting strife. Shane feels slightly nauseous however, remembering how he'd felt about this couple that night. He hated them. Their wealth. He remembers how he relished throwing them out and not serving them drinks. It was a small, but sweet, victory, good defeating evil. He thinks back now, and though the memory is clear, it's like something from a movie as opposed to Shane's own life. He's trying to piece together the events and emotions of the night as he would look back on a film after the credits rolled. Why did he hate them, exactly? What had they done to him? What exactly did he defeat them at? What battle were they waging, what game were they playing? Why was it a competition at all? How strange to be sharing wine with this couple, here, in his home, a year later.

"Luckily," Shane says, smiling, "we don't have any tequila. I'm not even sure we have glasses."

He heads to the kitchen and finds a corkscrew.

"Sorry I took a while to get here," he says from the open kitchen into the large living room. "No cold Pinot Grigio at the liquor store. Got Chardonnay."

"Ugh, you should have poured warm Pinot Grigio down the wine man's gullet, and then disemboweled him Braveheart-style," Everett says.

Zora looks at him. Shane stops pouring. Ashley giggles.

"He's kidding!" she says, whacking Everett on the arm. "Chardonnay is great. Stop scaring the neighbors, you jackhole."

Everett smiles like a naughty kid. Shane laughs and continues pouring.

"Warm Pinot Grigio would have been fine too," Everett says. "We're pretty easy. As long as it's wine!"

Shane distributes glasses to everyone, and Zora raises hers.

"Cheers!" she says, and they all clink glasses.

"Welcome to the neighborhood," Everett says. "The property taxes are ridiculous, but at least the schools are good. For public schools, anyway."

"You get what you pay for," Ashley says.

"I guess so," Shane says. "Which house are you guys in again?"

"Twenty-nine," Everett says. "On top of the hill."

"Oh," Shane says, taking a moment. "I… nice house."

"Hedge fund did well in 2013 when the real estate market up here dipped for a nanosecond," Everett says matter-of-factly. "We had a big stake in that pharma company that was researching toenail fungus and wound up curing prostate cancer instead. And Ashley's parents are Sharpie money. Sort of ridiculous. There are rooms in that house I've never been in."

"We lost a kid for a week and a half once," Ashley says.

Shane and Zora look at her skeptically.

"Kidding!" Ashley says. "It was only three days."

They all laugh and sip from their glasses. Shane is smiling and feeling relaxed. He thinks about the house on top of the hill. The one they just bought is six thousand square feet, but he's pretty sure it could fit inside number twenty-nine.

"Wow," Shane says. "I can't believe that's your house. I figured those owners would be—"

"Older?" Ashley asks.

"No…" Shane says, immediately wishing he hadn't opened his mouth.

"Douchier?" Everett asks, feigning insult. Zora snickers.

"Well, yeah." Shane says. "I guess. Sorry."

"We get that all the time," Everett says. "We are rich, yes, but we're not assholes. Just like many other rich, and poor, people aren't. I don't believe assholery… or is it assholedom? Ash?"

"Not sure," Ashley says, pulling out her phone. "I'll ask Siri."

"…is exclusive to the ranks of the rich," Everett continues. "It's an affliction that spans all economic strata."

"Siri," Ashley says into her phone. "Is it 'assholery' or 'assholedom'?"

Shane and Zora look on, amused, smiling, not exactly sure what to make of these two.

"Texas Hold 'Em," Siri says, "is a variation on the game of poker…"

"Oh, please," Ashley says, clicking her phone off, as everyone laughs.

"Hey," Everett says enthusiastically, taking a sip of wine, "one of the kids is having a birthday soon. Right, Ash? Which one?"

"Yes," Ashley says flatly. "Your son. Everett, Jr."

"What is he, like, four?" Everett asks.

"He's seven," Ashley says, staring at Everett. Zora and Shane try to stifle laughter.

"Anyway," Everett says, "You guys should come by next Saturday…"

"Sunday," Ashley says, shaking her head, looking skyward, sipping wine.

"Ashley's mom sets it all up," Everett continues, "the kids get bouncy castles and face painting and pizza and stuff. We get wine and a squadron of babysitters."

Shane and Zora look at each other with that new parent look that says, *That sounds really fun. Are we allowed to have fun?*

"Bring Hope," Everett continues, "she'll be out of your hands and in expert care for a few hours."

"Wow," Zora says. "You sure we can come?"

"Of course!" Ashley says. "I usually don't even know half the people at the kids' parties. What do you say?"

A big smile comes across Shane's face, and he feels more content than he has in a while.

"Yeah," he says. "That sounds really nice. Thanks."

"Mmm, this is good wine!" Ashley says, looking into her glass. "What is this?"

Shane shrugs sheepishly.

"Siri!" Ashley shouts at her phone. "What kind of wine is this?"

"I'm sorry," Siri says. "I can't taste."

"Well, fuck you then," Ashley says, as everyone cracks up.

CHAPTER 13

"The *union*?" Shane yells across his office to Jacob. "What does the union want?"

Jacob scrolls through the email they both received a moment ago from their employees, via an attorney for a local labor union. "Says they are concerned about 'Unfair Treatment,'" he says.

"What about how we are treating them is unfair?"

Jacob scrolls and reads for a moment. "Doesn't say."

"We pay more than any other packing facility in the state, right?"

"Yes. Probably in the country. Maybe the world."

"So what do they want?"

"More money," says Jacob. "Less hours, better benefits."

"Don't we all?" asks Shane. "Just demanding it, though, is just, well, greedy."

"Infuriatingly ironic, isn't it?" Jacob says.

"They are aware that they're free to mix up a batch of salad dressing that's so good it puts me out of business, and then open their own plants that pay a thousand dollars an hour, right?"

"I would assume so," Jacob says drily.

"And that there are thousands of higher paying jobs out there that they are welcome to go get any time?"

"Maybe they aren't qualified," Jacob counters, with an air of advocacy for the devil.

"So instead of becoming qualified and getting higher paying jobs, they'd rather *we* change the jobs they currently have into higher paying ones."

"Yes," Jacob says flatly.

"Why would we do that?"

"Because they'll strike if we don't."

"We can replace them all in an afternoon."

"You're worried about your rep in the press?" Jacob asks. "Watch what happens if you put all these guys on the street for 'just trying to support their families.' These unions have tons of power, and they know how to work the press and get public opinion on their side. They will have these guys and their wives and kids claiming we are starving them on that night's news."

"What about our families?" asks Shane.

"No one cares about our families."

"Why not?"

"Cuz we're rich."

"But this is just wrong," Shane says, gesturing at his computer screen. "It's… it's blackmail."

"The union calls it 'collective bargaining.'"

"What do we do?" Shane asks.

"Nothing we can do," Jacob says, resigned to the situation. "Just take it. Without lube."

"But we'll have to—"

"Produce less, expand less, hire less," Jacob interrupts. "Just be less. Like Detroit."

"So there will be less jobs here overall?"

"Again, infuriatingly ironic."

"Why would the union do this? I don't know the whole history, Norma Rae, Jimmy Hoffa and all that, but isn't the point of unions to protect workers from greedy bosses who force them to work long hours in dangerous conditions for low pay?"

"Maybe originally," Jacob says, "but not anymore."

"What? Why? What do you mean?"

"Some of the biggest, most powerful unions in the nation are the teachers' union and the police union."

"So?" Shane says.

"Who's the greedy boss *they* need protection from?"

"Well," Shane says, and thinks for a moment. "The government. Wait… those unions are protecting teachers and police from being taken advantage of by those we elect to protect us?"

"Bingo," Jacob says.

"That's insane," Shane says. "How is that legal?"

"Well, one reason, having nothing to do with protecting workers, is that the people making the laws, politicians, they like voters who vote in giant unified blocks. You get the unions on your side on Election Day, boom, victory. Anyone who threatens the unions will never win."

"And what's two?" Shane asks.

"You gonna complain about the unfairly swanky lifestyles of the guys with the guns and the folks who teach your children?"

"God," Shane says, defeated. "I never thought of that."

"Whatever life decisions the union leaders made, whatever environments they were raised in, it's all led them to an existence in which they don't create or produce anything. They gotta make a living somehow, so they make, market, and sell contempt. Just like Bristol and her website. It's their job. When we created something great," he says, and gestures around the processing plant, "we gave them an opportunity to create this." He points to the email on his screen. "Contempt is a cottage industry that keeps laborers, actors, government workers, lawyers and politicians rich."

Shane's phone buzzes: Sam.

"Yo, Sam. Please don't have bad news, I can't even today."

"Apple bought Toss," Sam says quickly.

Shane stands up, the phone pressed to his ear. Jacob looks across the office at him and raises an eyebrow.

"What?! No way!" Shane yells.

"Two. Hundred. Million. Dollars."

Shane's jaw drops, but he manages to create a wide-mouthed smile with it anyway.

"This is so awesome!" Sam says to Shane. "Love you, man."

"Oh, I love you too, you big jerk."

Shane and Sam emerge from a Manhattan nightclub, arms around each other, laughing and drunk. They stumble to the side of the front entrance. A bouncer looks at them, all muscles and disdain.

"And thanks for the ten million," Shane says.

"Damn, is that what I owe you?" Sam asks groggily. "Shit, that's a lot of scratch. Hope I still have it after that bar tab."

"You better," Shane says. "Hey, where's Gio?"

"Invited him," Sam says with a shrug. "I guess he couldn't make it."

Shane is disappointed, and is about to say something when a nerdy kid who looks like he came straight from ComiCon approaches the bouncer guarding the door. The kid and the bouncer start talking, and the volume of the conversation quickly rises to a level that gets Sam and Shane's attention.

"It's a fifty-dollar cover, kid," the bouncer says sternly.

"Come on, please?" the kid asks. "You made me wait for five hours. Can I please come in? Just for a minute."

"Fifty bucks," the bouncer says coldly.

"I only have forty," the kid says, looking into his Captain America wallet.

Sam gives Shane a look, and they walk over.

"Hey, man," Shane says to the kid. "What's up?"

"I'm here from Iowa on a chemistry fratority field trip."

"I'm sorry?" Sam asks.

"It's— forget it," the kid says. "I just turned twenty-one…" he looks at his Wolverine watch, "…thirteen minutes ago. I heard Robert Downey Jr. hangs out here sometimes, so I thought I'd go in. I came by at seven," he says, gesturing to the bouncer, "and this aggro mountain told me I had to wait till midnight. I did, and now he won't let me in!"

The bouncer scowls at him.

Shane says to the bouncer, "Hey, what gives?"

"He doesn't have the cover."

"How much is it?"

"Fifty."

"It was twenty an hour ago," Sam says.

The bouncer shrugs. "Inflation," he says, without a fuck to give.

Sam is about to say more when Shane holds up his hand to quiet him. He pulls out his wallet and removes two one-hundred-dollar bills.

"That should cover it," Shane says, handing the money to the kid. The kid looks at the money through two bespectacled swimming pools. "Happy birthday," Shane says.

Sam pulls out a money clip and peels off two more.

"Gotta buy a birthday drink," he says, handing them over. "They're crazy pricey. This ain't Iowa."

The bouncer shakes his head as the kid begins to vibrate with joy. "Holy shit! Who are you guys?"

"We're the Justice League," Sam says proudly, and Shane nods in agreement.

"Thank you!" the kid yells, overcome with nerd glee. "Holy sh— I mean, holy cow! I mean… thank you!"

"Now get in there and have a good time," Shane says, looking at the bouncer. "That is, if it's okay with you, sir?"

The bouncer grimaces, takes fifty bucks from the kid, and opens the ropes for him. The kid starts running toward the door.

"Hey!" Shane yells, stopping him in his tracks. "RDJ isn't in there."

"Shit," the kid says, dejected.

"But Scar-Jo is."

The kid looks as if he might have a nerdgasm.

"If you go upstairs, there's a private room entrance in the back, behind the DJ booth," Sam says. "Hang out there. She's gotta come out eventually. Don't be creepy."

"Oh my God! I won't," the kid says. "Thanks!"

The kid goes inside, and Shane and Sam stumble off, laughing proudly. The bouncer closes the ropes, as if to preserve what's left of his doorway fiefdom. Sam grabs his phone and sends a text.

"I gotta get a cab," Shane mumbles hazily. "Hope will be up screaming in…" He looks at his watch. "Now."

"Here's one," says Sam. Shane flags it down.

"Share?" Shane asks.

"Nah, Grand Central's the wrong direction. Besides, I'm set."

As the cab pulls over, the distinctive growl of a Lamborghini Aventador disrupts the still night air. As the orange land rocket approaches from 10th Avenue, it comes to a stop behind the cab, engine idling. A door opens vertically like the wing of a seven hundred horsepowered beetle. The driver steps out and says to Sam, "Ready, Mr. Mackle?"

Shane's mouth is in the shape of a capital "O."

"No. Friggin'. Way," he says.

"Oh yeah," Sam says, looking at the car like it's a newborn baby. "That's mine."

Shane takes a moment to check out the car, shamelessly gleaming under the streetlights. He listens to the primal metallic thunder of the engine. The cab driver has gotten out to admire the car, and is expressing his appreciation in his native tongue.

"You are *not* driving," Shane says.

"Noooo," Sam says, gesturing to the driver. "That's Phil. He comes with the car. Well, tonight anyway."

"Hey, Phil," Shane says.

Phil nods and smiles. Shane circles the car.

"You can touch it," Sam says. Shane runs his fingers over the meticulously polished paint.

"Wow. It feels... fast."

"We're only gonna be young, dumb, and rich once, right?"

"But... Jesus, Sam. What will people think?"

"They'll think I'm a huge asshole," Sam says, smiling. "With a small penis. And they'll be wrong. I absolutely am not an asshole."

"Sam," Shane says, laughing. "You don't need a car like this."

"You're damn right I don't. No one does. I don't even know how to drive it."

"Then why the hell would you buy it?" Shane asks.

"This car serves a very important purpose," Sam explains after a moment. "It's a signal to the Bristol Harts and union lawyers of the world that I DON'T GIVE A FUCK what they think of me. They can't use fear of public opinion against me. I went full asshole out of the gate, so they can't go sneaking around catching me doing what they perceive to be asshole behavior, like they do with you. They've got nothing to expose, so they will leave me alone. I drive a high octane neon sign that announces to the world, 'I am an asshole. Deal with it.'"

"You really are," Shane says, laughing.

"Did you have fun tonight?" Sam asks.

"Hell yeah."

"Think that power dork we got in will too?"

"Yes."

"Then I'm cool with being superhero of assholes."

He attempts to high five Shane, and they fail miserably, getting their arms tangled together spastically as if performing in a petit mal seizure-themed ballet. This launches into a ridiculous high-five epic failure, and an uncontrollable laughing fit. Phil and the cab driver are laughing too. The bouncer notices.

"Rich pricks," he mutters.

Zora enters the third extra bedroom, where Shane spent the night, a cup of coffee in her hand. She touches him gently on one arm.

"Hey," she says.

Shane stirs. His eyes pop open, and the pain this action causes is immediately apparent on his face. Zora winces in sympathy.

"You okay?" she asks quietly.

"Oh God," Shane says.

"You must feel awesome," she says. "Did you have fun?"

"Yes. Sorry," Shane says, rubbing his eyes, not sure exactly what he's apologizing for. "I got in late and didn't want to wake you." He looks around for his phone. "What time is it?"

"About ten. I let you sleep," Zora says, as Shane attempts to sit up. "One good thing about a big house. We stayed in the western sector all morning so you wouldn't hear a thing."

"Oh," Shane says, attempting a smile. "Thanks."

"It's not every day your friend makes two hundred million dollars," Zora says, handing the coffee mug to Shane.

"Thanks," he says, and tries to drown the cobwebs with a healthy swig. "Can you believe it? Crazy."

"Completely. Hey, you left your phone in the kitchen. It's been buzzing," she says. "A lot."

She pulls the phone from her pocket and hands it to Shane. He hits a button and looks at it, a bit worried he'll see a MeMeMe headline about a nerd incident involving Scarlett Johansson. What he does see causes his hangover to immediately intensify with the onset of anger.

"Jesus Christ!" he yells at the phone. "I want off this roller coaster, I swear! They have got to be kidding."

"Calm down," Zora says soothingly. "What now?"

He hands her the phone. She looks at it. MeMeMe is running an article featuring a picture of Shane and Sam from the previous night, standing next to the Lamborghini in an embarrassing drunken high five. Under the picture is the caption: *"Local Food Dude Parties Hard with Software Millionaire."*

"Wow. That's not even... anything right. At all," Zora says. "Whose car is that?"

"Sam's," he says to a wide-eyed Zora. "But he's a genius. That stupid car takes away their ability to tell the story they want to tell, that he's a rich asshole."

"But he's sorta acting like one," Zora observes.

"It doesn't matter. It worked. He's in complete control of how the world perceives him, no matter what the reality. I have no control. I drive a CR-V, and this article is about one rich asshole. Me. They're accusing me of what, having fun?

Greed? He bought the Lamborghini and I'm greedy. What the fuck?"

"I don't think it's that," Zora says, hesitantly. "They're wrong, of course, but I think the story they're selling is that you're a hypocrite."

"A hypocrite?" Shane asks. "How?"

"Well, you were the hero of the anti-capitalists, slinging drinks to throngs of liberal Bushwick hipsters at the bar, and now you're in Westchester with the big house, the SUV, the thriving business, and the rich friends. It looks like you're not being true to your roots."

"What roots? I wasn't successful, now I am. This is a personal flaw? The house, the car, Sam's app? Those things just sort of… happened. They had to. If that's hypocrisy, it's hypocrisy of necessity."

"Yes, I know. Of course," Zora says. "It's like… natural. Destiny, you could say. It's not really hypocrisy at all. It's just behavior that some people don't agree with. So much for tolerance."

"Well, maybe I don't agree with *their* behavior," Shane says, with resolve. "And I've just about had it."

"Shane, you're hungover. Have some coffee."

"I'm fine, Zo. I've just finally realized that I can either continue to get shit on and lied about, or do something about it. I'm tired of getting shit on. These people want me to be an asshole, I can arrange that."

CHAPTER 14

"Okay, Sam," one of the team of lawyers says. "Just sign these, and the deal is officially done."

Shane, Jacob, Sam, and four attorneys are gathered around a large conference table in a midtown law office, shuffling through a neat stack of papers.

The lawyer places a page in front of Sam. He signs, and smiles at Shane. Shane smiles back.

"Congratulations, Mr. Mackle," the lawyer says. "You are now an official owner of the entity formally known as 'Citizen Shane's Ramp Spritz,' currently functioning under the DBA umbrella, 'YakSpritz, Inc.'"

"Well, thank you very much," Sam says, as he shakes hands with Shane, and then Jacob.

"Congratulations," Shane says. "I wish you guys the best. Hey, how's the union thing going?"

"Well," Jacob says, "I brought Sam to the plant to give the workers a presentation as part of our new continuing education program, per the union mandate to enrich the lives of our employees."

"Oh, really?" Shane asks.

"Yep," Sam replies. "I used some of my tech skills and the two hundred mil to put together a badass PowerPoint demo: 'The Future of Food.'

"It was amazing," says Jacob. "The video was able to show how in the future, every one of the workers in the plant would be replaced with robots. Very informative."

"Very educational," Sam adds. "And sexy. I got one of the Real Housewives of New Jersey editors to cut it."

"And you know," Jacob adds, "we got an email from the union lawyer that afternoon, saying the workers had decided to rescind their demands and threats to unionize. Really strange."

"Totally," Shane says, smiling.

"Good work, partner," Jacob says to Sam.

"Thank you, sir," Sam says.

"Now come on," Shane says, smiling. "We have a plane to catch."

CHAPTER 15

Zora and Hope (who's walking now), Henry and his wife and son, Everett and Ashley and their kids, Jacob, and a few others are being greeted and led onto a private jet by Shane, Sam, and some of the jet's staff. Everyone exchanges hellos, and happily boards the plane. Shane smiles proudly as he stands at the bottom of the steps leading to the plane's door, looks toward the airport's terminal building, and scowls slightly.

"I think it's time, my friend," Sam says, as he heads in.

"Yeah," Shane says.

As he gazes across the bleak, gray tarmac of the private airfield in Teterboro, New Jersey, he thinks about the past two years and the surreal roller coaster ride it has been. While the visible, material changes in Shane's life are obvious—the money, the house, the family—there's a bigger change in Shane that's not quite as apparent. He's learned more in the past two years than he ever thought possible. He wasn't even trying to learn anything. He thought he had it all figured out. Now here he is, a man he didn't know two years ago, standing on a private airfield with a jet full of hedge fund, software, and culinary millionaires behind him. Two years ago, he would have hoped for the plane to crash. Now he's thrilled and proud to be boarding it.

Looking back, he sees that he hadn't even known what he didn't know; about business, of course, but so much more than that. He used to see the world through a specific lens, one ground from a philosophy that made things look clear and focused on the surface but held ugly scratches and deep imperfections upon further inspection. Now, it's as if someone not only wiped the lens clean, but gave him an all new camera. He now sees the world as a screwed-up place, and the people in it screwed-up creatures, but his new perspective has also given him the cognitive and moral foundation, as well as the confidence, to understand and manage it all. He can't believe all the years of school that didn't get him anywhere close to where he is now, having now experienced this new facet of life. He looks back on his old attitude with embarrassment, disdain, childish innocence, and ignorance. As messy a place as the world is, Shane now finds beauty in his new perspective, a better world than he knew before. A full frame DSLR can capture images of horrific and ugly things, but they will always be clearer and more satisfying than those from a Polaroid.

He looks southeast to the New York City skyline, the buildings reaching toward the sky, and realizes that they look different now. He used to see a glass and steel collective symbol of wealth, greed, and heartlessness. Now, even from this great distance he sees each individual building as a dream.

Each colossal structure, one man's dream, fulfilled. Each a testament to years or even decades of work, effort, wisdom, perseverance and diligence. He thinks of the challenges he's faced just getting some seasoned olive oil into homes and restaurants around the world, and can't imagine the insurmountable odds these men who broke through the earth and created these massive places of residence, business, and entertainment must have overcome.

People needed and wanted these buildings, but he knows from experience how little appreciation must have been shown to those who built them. People come to love things like buildings, cars, and amusement parks, yet they vilify those who create them. Why?

Because of money.

Shane wonders if the masses would stop hating the rich and productive if only they would produce buildings, cars and amusement parks for free. He then realizes that this is not worth contemplating, because without the promise of money as a reward, there would be no buildings, cars, or amusement parks to use and enjoy. Those opposed to wealth accumulation would say that they are not actually opposed to people making money for producing things, so long as it's not "too much" money. And who are the judges of what qualifies as "too much"? Those who don't have as much as they want. And that's the heart of the problem. Money had become not so much a quantifiable tool of measuring productivity and reward, but a thing whose acceptable level of possession was decided by those who wished they had more of it. How much money did Shane Foster deserve? Shane had come to conclude that the question was not only irrelevant and impossible to answer, but offensive. The people who would claim that material possessions are not important to a person's integrity are the same to judge someone's virtue *solely* on their material possessions. Sam was right. It didn't matter what he felt, thought, cared about, or did in life. Orange Lamborghini equals asshole. Orange Lamborghinis didn't really exist for those looking to drive a high-performance Italian sports car. They were a sign that said, "I know your stupid game, I'm not playing, and I win." Shane's last remaining doubt on the issue was erased when he read a story in the local Westchester paper about a protest taking place in front of a local billionaire's house. The townspeople were upset that this billionaire wasn't ignoring a debt some sad dysfunctional third world tyranny owed him. Shane read the article, rife with quotes from the townspeople about generosity, forgiveness, and the importance being a good neighbor. But then he did a little research into the billionaire himself, who, as the protestors and the media who love them continually ignore, is an actual individual person. This individual was a scientist originally, and had amassed his fortune by applying his genius-level mathematical skills to the stock market. At some point, he left his hedge fund to his partners and built a supercomputer that was currently in the process of figuring out a cure for cancer. CANCER. How much better a neighbor did these people want than a neighbor who was curing cancer? How much money does someone curing cancer "deserve?" You had to dig deep into the Internet to find this individual's background information, but the story of the protesters who woke up and decided that this man had "too much money" was front page news. If dedicating your life to curing cancer couldn't shield you from the scorn of the financially unfulfilled, nothing could. Shane sighs.

No wonder everyone hates everyone.

Money may be the root of all evil, but only in that most people don't understand its fundamental purpose and function: to universally quantify, motivate, and reward the good that can be done by the humans who share space on a rock hurtling through space at sixty thousand miles per hour.

Before the dawn of civilization, "goodness" was equivalent to power. The more raw power an individual had, the more easily he could acquire life's necessities and luxuries, and care for and protect his loved ones. The introduction of currency made it possible to acquire these things without the utilization of force. Money brought peace and order to a brutal and violent world. It was the essence of, and conduit to, what we call "civilization." People don't understand this, and they fear and hate that which they don't understand. Therefore they steer the world onto a course of self-destruction. Not allowing currency to perform its intended purpose as a means of distributing limited resources amongst society peacefully will cause a natural reversal back to what humanity once was: a ruthless arena in which only the most evil and most powerful rise and rule.

Are there rich people who exploit their ability to create wealth to the detriment of others? Of course. Are there those who exploit their *lack* of ability to the same extent? Which is worse? In the past two years, Shane saw that the pervasive attitude in society was vilification of those with the ability to create wealth, and championing of those without it, regardless of the individual morals, motivations, and merits of those being judged. He noticed that the only wealthy members of society that received universal love and praise were musicians, athletes, and movie stars.

Shane shakes his head and smiles at the thought of it. Who would have thought that some salad spritz, a girl named Zora, and a baby named Hope would have taught him how wrong he was about so much, not so very long ago? He pulls his Canon 5D from his shoulder bag, points it towards the skyline, focuses, and shoots.

"Beautiful," he says, checking the shot in the camera's preview screen.

Ignorance certainly was bliss, but knowledge is truly divine.

"Mr. Foster," the head flight attendant says from the plane door. "Alright if we close up? Don't want to delay the flight."

"I know," says Shane quietly. "Just… just one more minute."

"Okay," says the attendant. "I'll get everyone settled."

Shane stares across the airfield and checks his watch. He turns to board, and then does a double take. He looks back toward the terminal building and sees Gio exiting a door and running onto the tarmac with a uniformed airport attendant, who is emphatically pointing the way to the plane. Gio is headed in the right direction. Shane smiles.

"Hey," Gio says as he reaches the plane.

"Glad you made it," Shane says.

"I almost didn't."

"Still mad at me?" Shane asks.

"What?" Gio asks, somewhat surprised. "No. I'm pretty embarrassed is all."

"Embarrassed? Why? You definitely shouldn't be. Sorry if I made you feel that way."

"No. I'm sorry. You were right. I got out of the music game. I wasn't good at it. I'm looking for a marketing gig."

"Oh," Shane says, happily surprised. "That sounds good, man. I'll keep an ear out for you if you like. But, for now, this week is about enjoying ourselves. No work allowed! Ready to have some fun?"

"Yeah," Gio says quietly, fidgeting with his bag. "I mean… yeah, let's go."

"What?" Shane asks, concerned.

"It's just… you guys are all millionaires," Gio says. "I'm an unemployed musician. It's embarrassing. But I didn't want to leave it the way we did. So, I was glad to get the invite. I'll try to fit in."

Shane stands in front of Gio and puts his hand on his shoulder. It's clear that Gio doesn't want to be there, that he came only to avoid further damage to their relationship.

"Gio," Shane says. "It's me, man. I'm the same guy from behind the bar. So's Sam. And everyone else is way cool too. You will like them and they will love you. Being rich doesn't mean you're different than not rich people, and it certainly doesn't mean you're better. It doesn't make life all fucking awesome all the time either, believe me. It's just different kinds of bullshit you have to deal with. The worst part about it is how it makes people look at you, feel about you, and how it fucks up friendships. That's not worth any amount of money. Make sense?"

Gio looks up at Shane after a moment and smiles.

"Yeah, man, it does," he says. "Thanks."

"Now come on," Shane says, patting him vigorously on the back. "There's an island with our name on it."

Gio smiles broadly and nods his head as they board the plane.

"Hey, everyone," Shane says as he enters. "I have some bad news. Anyone who thought they were the coolest guy on the plane is wrong, because the G-Man is here!"

Gio enters a step behind Shane, and waves sheepishly.

"Yes!" Sam yells. "Fu… Fun times ahead! Fun, yeah!" He adjusts his expression of excitement as he notices all the kids on the plane.

There are some surprised faces, but everyone is happy to see Gio. They wave and say hello. Gio hands his bag off to an attendant and finds a seat, as Shane makes his way to the front of the plane near the cockpit and addresses the group.

"Thanks so much, all of you, for joining Zora and me. We will be taking off momentarily."

"Where the fu—" Sam catches himself mid-sentence again. "Where are we going, Mr. Mysterious?"

Shane smiles and continues.

"We are headed to a small island in the Bahamas that will be all ours for the week. We've got meals all set, adventures and activities for kids, and adults as well. I felt a little celebration was in order for the sale of my stake in the business to Sam, Jacob's new partner, Henry's new bar, all these kids who look like they're ready to have good time, and everyone else's accomplishments. I know we all have a lot of work to do in the real world, but I thought it was time for a little compulsory fun."

The passengers are smiling with glee. Shane continues, "Oh, almost forgot!" He holds up his left hand. "Zo and I got married."

The crowd gasps, offers congratulations, and looks for Zora. No one can find her.

"I know she got on. Zo?" Shane asks, looking around, on the verge of concern, when a hand rises into view from behind a row of seats toward the tail, adorned with a dazzling four-carat diamond. The rest of Zora is obscured from view, as she's ducking behind a seat.

"Thanks!" she says from behind the seat. "Hope shat."

Everyone laughs and cheers.

"I love you, sweetie," says Shane. "There's a nanny on the island, I promise. Several, actually. Yes, so, thanks everyone. It's a wedding and honeymoon of sorts as well. Zora and I couldn't think of a better way to celebrate than with you guys. Champagne's coming around!"

Flight attendants materialize with flutes of champagne to hand out to everyone. When everyone has a glass, Shane holds his up.

"Please join me for a toast," he says, as everyone raises their glasses. "To all—" He stops suddenly. "Oh wait, you know what, hold on a sec. Before I forget, there is one more thing I need to do. Excuse me, just one second."

The crowd watches curiously as Shane pulls out his phone, dials, and holds it to his ear, smiling.

"Hello. Is this Bristol? Hello, Bristol, Shane Foster here…"

The people on the plane stare in disbelief.

"Yes, it's really me… Crazy, I know… No, no, don't be silly. I actually have a scoop for you, since you like writing about me so much and all. Yes, I do… I'm switching careers. I'm a philanthropist now. Or humanitarian. Or environmentalist. Any of those should work for you, right? Pick one… Oh, and a journalist. My first piece is on power and privilege, and it's going to be in MeMeMe actually. Yes… what? Oh, I know… how? Well… because I bought it."

"No!" Jacob says with a proud smile.

"Oh yeah," Sam says, as Shane continues.

"Yeah, the whole company. From your dad, who's the real owner, I came to find out. Said something about your 'lack of appreciation' at the final sale meeting. He wishes you luck. Yes… I know, cray. Became official at noon today. We're going to focus more on positive pieces about many of the people you've written about in the past… you know people who actually produce and do stuff. Yes… I'm very excited about the future direction of the company. Unfortunately, you won't be a part of it, because you're fired."

He hangs up. After a moment, everyone on the plane bursts into cheers and laughter. Shane maneuvers through the aisles to hug Zora and Hope.

"That feel good?" Zora asks.

"Yes!" Shane says, then addresses the crowd and crew. "Let's fly!"

CHAPTER 16

Somebody said to me, 'But the Beatles were anti-materialistic.' That's a huge myth. John and I literally used to sit down and say, "Now let's write a swimming pool."

– Paul McCartney

Colorful drinks flow as the adults watch the kids splashing and playing water volleyball with some lifeguard/babysitters in the pool outside a luxurious oceanside resort. Two more sitters are playing games with Hope and two other toddlers under a shade near a baby pool. Shane and Zora are strolling on the beach nearby.

"God, this is beautiful," Zora says, looking at the ocean.

"Yes. It is," Shane says, looking at her.

"Stop," Zora says.

"No."

Zora instinctively tries to cover up, but quickly realizes how difficult that is to do in a bikini. She whacks Shane in the stomach as an alternative.

"This is kind of perfect," Zora says. "I hope everyone's having a good time."

Just then, a giant splash and shrieks of glee are heard from the pool. Shane and Zora smile.

"I think they are," Shane says. "I'm guessing that was Jacob demonstrating the Yak-Cannonball."

"This was a great idea," Zora says, laughing.

"Which part?"

"The trip. Selling the business. Marrying me. All of it."

"Easy decisions all. Happiness isn't easy. But it's a lot easier with you," Shane says. "I love you."

"Me too," Zora says, and they kiss.

"And thank you," Shane says.

Zora looks at him, confused. "For what?" she asks.

"For pushing me to go where I didn't want to go. You were right."

"Hey, you did it all yourse—"

"No. No, I didn't," he interrupts. "Trust me, if it weren't for you, I would still be tending bar, doing nothing important, thinking I was happy. Thank you for opening my eyes, and literally giving me a new life."

Zora looks at Shane. There certainly have been times over the past two years when she wasn't sure she made the right choice in Citizen Shane Foster. This was not one of them.

"Okay," she says, "I'll admit that I was secretly nudging you toward the light. But only because I cared. I saw something in you. You were already someone special. Someone I was attracted to. Someone I wanted to share this journey with, play this crazy game of life with, and win. And you turned out to be the best teammate anyone could ask for."

"We do make a pretty good team," Shane says.

"We kick ass," Zora says, as they kiss again.

"We better get back," Shane says, taking Zora's hand and walking toward the pool, "before people start talking."

"About what?" Zora says, holding up her ring finger. "We're married."

"Oh yeah. I forgot."

Zora smacks him on the arm.

The ladies are getting poolside massages while Shane, Sam, Henry, Jacob, Everett and Gio sit at a table under an umbrella, smoking cigars and chatting. Gio looks a little timid. His eyes are darting around amid the banter, seeking an opportunity to join in, but he's finding it difficult.

"You know what the best thing about places like this is?" Everett says.

"Everything," says Sam.

"It's the smell," Everett says, inhaling deeply. "Can you smell that? You can't fake that. You have to spend a lot of money, just to smell that smell."

The guys start fervently sniffing the air, clearing cigar smoke with waving hands to get at it. Zora and Ashley look over to them and giggle.

"It's a mixture of coconuts, rum, and awesome," Henry says.

"I would pay a lot of money to take that home," Jacob says. "Mmm."

"That would be cool," Shane says.

"Like air fresheners," Jacob says.

"They have those," Sam says. "But they always smell like air fresheners."

The guys sit for a moment, contemplating life and the smell of the island. Everett breaks the smoky silence.

"What if you took the time, did the research, and actually sampled the local flowers and foliage and stuff, collected genuine exotic smells…"

"Bottled them up and sold them…" Henry says.

"Laundry sheets, candles…" Jacob adds.

"At tourist shops on the same islands where the smells originated…" Sam says.

"Island Essence," Shane says, moving his hand as if outlining a label on an invisible bottle of a non-existent product.

There is a pause as all the guys contemplate a simmering collective notion. A breeze finds its way from the warm Atlantic waters to the table and clears away the haze of cigar smoke.

"You CAN Take It With You," Gio says meekly.

The guys all look at each other. Shane raises an eyebrow. He smiles and nods approvingly at Gio, who smiles from ear to ear.

THE END

www.ingramcontent.com/pod-product-compliance
Lightning Source LLC
Chambersburg PA
CBHW020255030426
42336CB00010B/772